FRANCE
in Pictures

VGS

Alison Behnke

Twenty-First Century Books

Contents

Lerner Publishing Group, Inc., realizes that current information and statistics quickly become out of date. To extend the usefulness of the Visual Geography Series, we developed www.vgsbooks.com, a website offering links to up-to-date information, as well as in-depth material, on a wide variety of subjects. All the websites listed on www.vgsbooks.com have been carefully selected by researchers at Lerner Publishing Group, Inc. However, Lerner Publishing Group, Inc., is not responsible for the accuracy or suitability of the material on any website other than www.lernerbooks.com. It is recommended that students using the Internet be supervised by a parent or teacher. Links on www.vgsbooks.com will be regularly reviewed and updated as needed.

Website address: www.lernerbooks.com

Twenty-First Century Books
A division of Lerner Publishing Group, Inc.
241 First Avenue North
Minneapolis, MN 55401 U.S.A.

web enhanced @ www.vgsbooks.com

CULTURAL LIFE 46

► Religion. Holidays and Festivals. Literature. Art
and Architecture. Music. Performing Arts and
Film. Food. Sports.

THE ECONOMY 58

► Services and Trade. Manufacturing and
Industry. Agriculture. Fishing and Forestry.
Mining and Energy. Transportation. Media and
Communications. The Future.

FOR MORE INFORMATION

Library of Congress Cataloging-in-Publication Data

Behnke, Alison.
      France in pictures / by Alison Behnke.
          p.   cm. – (Visual geography series. Second series)
      Includes bibliographical references and index.
      ISBN 978-0-8225-2675-9 (lib. bdg. : alk. paper)
      1. France—Juvenile literature. I. Title.
   DC17.B42 2011
   944—dc22   2009033893

Manufactured in the United States of America
1 - BP - 7/15/10

INTRODUCTION

France—officially called the French Republic—is a large and populous nation in Western Europe. The country has been an artistic center and a crossroads of trade for two thousand years. It has a coastline on the Atlantic Ocean and the Mediterranean Sea and a varied landscape of mountains and rolling fields. During its history, the nation has attracted settlers—and invaders—from areas that later became Italy, Germany, Norway, and more.

A series of kings and queens ruled the country for centuries. During that time, these rulers built a powerful colonial empire in many different regions of the world. At its height, the French Empire extended to North America, Africa, Asia, and islands in the Pacific Ocean. But royal rule ended with the French Revolution in the late 1700s. After bringing down Europe's richest monarchy, the French Revolution led to political shifts in France and in other parts of the European continent.

France's standing among its fellow European nations also changed during the 1800s. Profits from trade became more important than

4

territorial expansion, and competition for new markets often caused
conflicts between France and its neighbors. As trade grew in France,
so did industry. Factory workers in French cities became a powerful
group. These laborers influenced governments with their support or
opposition.

In the 1800s and 1900s, a series of wars between France and
Germany caused great damage and killed many people. Two major
conflicts—World War I (1914–1918) and World War II (1939–1945)—
brought challenges and great suffering. By the mid-twentieth century,
many French colonies had won their independence, ending France's
overseas empire.

The challenges did not end with the end of the twentieth century.
In the modern era, the French have faced the difficulties of adapting
to the European Union (EU). This organization has worked to unify
the continent's economic markets by lifting trade barriers and creat-
ing a common currency, the euro. While the EU offers benefits, it also

requires changes from its member nations. For example, France replaced its traditional currency, the franc, with the euro.

The large number of immigrants who have arrived in the country since the mid-twentieth century also challenges French society. Many of these immigrants come from France's former colonies in North Africa. The culture of these residents sometimes clashes with French traditions. In addition, many immigrant families live in poverty, and they often face discrimination in their new country. These situations have created unrest and sometimes violence.

NEAR AND FAR

In addition to its main body of land in Europe, France holds several overseas departments and territories. They include French Guiana in South America, French Polynesia in the South Pacific Ocean, Réunion in the Indian Ocean, and Martinique in the Caribbean Sea.

Amid many changes and upheavals, the French people continue to take great pride in their country's history, culture, and achievements. France remains a leader in industry, agriculture, and science. French is an international language in business, politics, and science. And people around the globe admire French writers, architects, and painters. Paris, the nation's capital, is home to some of the most renowned art museums in the world. France is also internationally famous for filmmaking and fashion, as well as for fine food and wine. Millions of visitors come to France every year to experience and enjoy all that the nation has to offer.

Moving into the future, French leaders seek to balance the many facets of their country. In particular, they must address their people's desire to preserve French identity and culture, while also achieving economic strength and good political relations with the rest of Europe and the world.

Visit www.vgsbooks.com for links to websites offering current news about France's politics, economy, and culture.

THE LAND

Lying in Western Europe, France covers an area of 211,209 square miles (547,029 square kilometers). The nation is about twice the size of the U.S. state of Colorado. France is roughly six-sided in shape, with its longest distance from north to south measuring about 600 miles (966 km). The country's greatest width from east to west is about 550 miles (885 km).

Most of France's borders run along natural barriers formed by mountains or water. The Pyrénées Mountains separate France from Spain and Andorra to the south. The Alps form France's frontier with Italy in the southeast, and the Jura Mountains line the border with Switzerland in the east. To the northeast lie Germany, Luxembourg, and Belgium.

Three seas also make natural boundaries for France. The Mediterranean Sea touches the country's southern coast. The English Channel—called La Manche in French—separates northwestern France from England. The Bay of Biscay, an arm of the Atlantic Ocean, stretches along the western coast. Sand dunes, marshes, rocky headlands, deep bays, and high limestone cliffs line many of the country's shores.

The island of Corsica is also French. It lies in the Mediterranean Sea about 100 miles (161 km) off France's southeastern coast. In addition, France continues to rule territories in the Caribbean Sea, in the Indian and Pacific oceans, and in South America.

Topography

France's topography, or landscape, is varied, especially in altitude. The seven major topographical regions are the Brittany-Normandy Hills, the Paris Basin, the Northeastern Plateaus, the Aquitaine Lowlands, the Pyrénées, the Eastern Mountains, and the Massif Central.

The Brittany-Normandy Hills of northwestern France make up a low, rolling, region that stretches to the English Channel and Atlantic Ocean. Toward the east, the broad, large Paris Basin is a plains region that occupies much of north-central France. North of the Paris Basin lie the flat lowlands of the Northeastern Plateaus. This region extends to the Belgian border and includes Flanders, a mining region.

The Aquitaine Lowlands in southwestern France comprise another region of plains. This area extends southwards from the central Loire River Valley to the Pyrénées Mountains.

The Pyrénées rise along the French border with Spain. Some of this range's peaks reach more than 11,000 feet (3,353 meters) above sea level. The mountains have historically prevented easy trade and transportation between France and Spain. Few passes cut through the Pyrénées.

Other major peaks make up the Eastern Mountains. The most important range in this region is the French Alps. Beginning near Nice, a city on the Mediterranean coast, the French Alps reach France's border with Switzerland. Located in the French Alps are many of Europe's highest peaks, including Mont Blanc. At 15,771 feet (4,807 m) above sea level, Mont Blanc is the tallest point in France—and in the Alps. Several high mountain valleys near Mont Blanc contain glaciers. These slow-moving masses of ice have gradually carved valleys through the Alps over many thousands of years.

Smaller ranges in the Eastern Mountains include the Jura Mountains, which lie along the French-Swiss border. The Vosges Mountains in the northeast have forested slopes and grassy, rounded summits.

A handful of other ranges occupy the Massif Central, a high plateau in south-central France. Many extinct volcanoes dot the massif's plateaus.

◉ Rivers

The winding rivers of northern and western France have long been important trade and transportation routes. Some of these rivers flow west toward the Atlantic Ocean. Other waterways empty into the Mediterranean Sea. An extensive network of human-made canals links these river systems. The canals also connect France with inland water routes in other European countries.

The main river of this complex network is the 485-mile-long (781 km) Seine. The Seine flows through France's northern

The Seine River flows through Paris. Tourists can get a good look at the city by taking one of the many riverboat sightseeing tours. Thirty-seven bridges cross the Seine in Paris alone.

The Château de Chenonceau, built in the early 1500s, sits where the Cher River meets the Loire River. Two earlier castles, each destroyed in the 1400s, previously occupied the spot.

plains and empties into the English Channel near the port of Rouen. Barges carrying coal and other products share this busy river with private houseboats and water taxis. About two thousand years ago, settlers founded France's capital city of Paris on several small islands in a wide spot in the Seine. Many secondary rivers, or tributaries, flow into the Seine. The Marne and Oise rivers arrive from the northern region of Flanders. The Eure and Yonne rivers join the Seine from the southeast.

Throughout central France flows the wide, shallow Loire River. This waterway rises in the southern Massif Central plateau. It then flows 634 miles (1,020 km) to the north and west before entering the Bay of Biscay near the city of Nantes. It is the nation's longest waterway. The Loire is famous for the chateaus (country houses and castles) and vineyards built along its banks. Large boats and barges cannot use the Loire, because of its many islands and its often shallow gravel banks.

Another river known for the castles along its course is the Rhine. It begins in western Switzerland and forms a portion of France's border with Germany. The Moselle River, a tributary of the Rhine, lies almost entirely within France. The Moselle, Meuse, and Escaut rivers all link the nation with ports on the North Sea. This body of water lies north of the Netherlands and Germany, east of the United Kingdom, and southwest of Norway. The Rhine River empties into the North Sea. In southern France, the Rhône River was once a rapid and wild river. But a series of dams that provide power and irrigation (water for fields) have tamed the river to some extent. At the mouth of the Rhône, near Marseille, lies a saltwater marsh called La Camargue.

Climate

France's climate varies depending on distance from the sea. Along the Atlantic coast, winds from the ocean moderate temperatures in both summer and winter. Coastal and northern areas have a rainy climate year-round. The annual rainfall in cities along the English Channel ranges from about 39 to 47 inches (99 to 119 centimeters).

Farther inland—in Paris and the Paris Basin—summers are warmer and rainfall levels are lower. Paris has temperatures that average approximately 39°F (4°C) in January (the coldest month). July is the hottest month, with an average temperature of about 65°F (18°C). Paris receives about 25 inches (64 cm) of rain throughout the year. Overall, central and eastern France have warmer summers and colder winters than coastal areas.

Elevation also affects regional climate. Winters are cold in the Massif Central and in the mountainous border regions. In the Alpine town of Embrun, for example, January temperatures average about 33°F (0.6°C). In July they hover around 67°F (19°C). These highland areas receive an average of more than 40 inches (102 cm) of precipitation per year. At lower elevations in the east, rains are heaviest in summer. In winter the mountains get much of their precipitation as snow.

To the south, a Mediterranean climate prevails. Summers are hot and winters are mild, while rainfall is low. During the winter, the Alps block cold weather from the region. At Marseille, a Mediterranean port, temperatures average 45°F (7.2°C) in January and about 73°F (23°C) in July. Annual rainfall averages about 22 inches (56 cm). Cool northerly winds called mistrals blow through central France and over the Mediterranean coast, especially during the winter and spring. These winds sometimes cause crop damage.

Flora and Fauna

France still has many of its original forests, which cover about one-fourth of the country's total land area. Walnut, oak, chestnut, beech, and ash trees grow in central and southern France. Poplars line many French highways, as well as smaller roads running from village to village. Pine forests thrive on mountain slopes. In southern France, olive trees and tall, thin cypresses flourish in the dry, warm climate. Lichens and mosses grow in the mountains at elevations too high for trees.

A WALK IN THE PARK

Hundreds of years ago, French laws set aside some of the country's forests for wealthy people. They hunted the many animals that roamed in the reserved woodlands. In modern times, all French citizens can enjoy these reserves. Parts of them are hiking retreats, while others remain game parks for hunting.

The wild horses of La Camargue charge across the sandy beaches of this saltwater marsh in southern France.

FIDO'S DISTANT COUSIN

One of France's most unusual animals is the raccoon dog. Originally from Asia, the raccoon dog was introduced in Europe in the early to mid 1900s. The animals spread quickly and now roam much of present-day Europe. These creatures are related to dogs but look very similar to raccoons. Raccoon dogs are nocturnal (active at night) and shy. They generally prefer to live in forests, where their long, curved claws help them climb trees. They are omnivorous, meaning that they eat meat as well as plants. Depending on what's available, their diet includes everything from toads and spiders to berries and other fruit. They sometimes play dead to stay safe from enemies.

Centuries of farming, hunting, and settlement have reduced France's population of large mammals. But deer and foxes still inhabit some forests and plains. Wolves, bears, and a few wild boars survive in remote mountains, particularly in the Pyrénées. The chamois—a large, agile animal resembling an antelope—climbs the slopes of the Alps. The small, catlike genet is a shy creature that hunts rodents at night in French forests. The unusual raccoon dog also favors a home in the forest or along a river or lake. This animal is in the dog family but resembles a raccoon and often fishes for its dinner. Wild rabbits hop through the French countryside, especially in the north. Porcupines, weasels, red squirrels, pheasants, and wild turkeys flourish in less populated regions of the nation.

Some of Europe's last surviving wild horses live in La Camargue. Cranes, herons, and other migrating birds also live in this area.

Freshwater fish inhabit France's lakes and waterways. Fishing for pike, bass, and perch in lakes is a popular sport, and fishers cast for trout in France's mountain streams.

Natural Resources and Environmental Challenges

France has a variety of natural resources, but few of them exist in large amounts. However, the nation has earned income by mining its various minerals. Coal and iron-ore deposits in northern France have boosted industry in that region. Deposits of other metals and minerals also contribute to the country's earnings. For example, bauxite (from which aluminum is made), potash (used in agriculture and industry), lead, and uranium are all present.

France has long depended heavily on oil and natural gas imports for energy. Some oil deposits do exist within the nation's borders, but they are small. Similarly, limited natural gas reserves once existed, but the country has used up much of this resource.

As part of an effort to import less fuel, the nation is a leading developer of nuclear power. France imports uranium, an element used in the production of nuclear energy, to power its nuclear reactors. France's many rivers offer another source of energy through hydroelectric power.

Like other industrialized nations, France faces environmental challenges. The nation's rivers, streams, and lakes suffer from water pollution due to industry and agriculture. Air pollution is also a problem, caused in part by heavy vehicle traffic, especially in Paris. Acid rain and toxic waste disposal are other ongoing issues.

The French government has worked to address these problems. National laws impose fines and other punishments on polluters. The country's leaders have also set aside protected land in parks and nature reserves. These areas help conserve endangered animals and plants. At-risk animals in France include the Mediterranean monk seal, the long-fingered bat, and the Pyrenean desman (a semiaquatic, molelike mammal).

ON THIN ICE

In recent decades, climate change has brought rising temperatures around the globe. France has not been immune to these changes. The glaciers that have carved out so many of the nation's alpine valleys have begun to melt. Some scientists predict that if the trend continues, these glaciers could be nearly gone by 2050. Their loss could lead to shortages of drinking water and water for crops, as well as hurt France's skiing industry and other tourism.

◉ Cities

France's capital and largest city is Paris, which lies along the Seine River in the nation's northern plains. The city and its surrounding suburbs have a total population of more than 10.5 million—about one-sixth of France's 62 million people. It is the center of the French national government. It is also the country's cultural, financial, and educational heart. The city's many museums and sights attract artists and tourists. Most Parisians have jobs in industry or in the service sector, which includes tourism, banking, and communications.

Paris's Louvre art museum is the world's largest museum in area, covering more than 100 acres (40 hectares).

PARIS has been the French capital since the tenth century. Many of its buildings date back to the eighteenth and nineteenth centuries. The French Empire was at its height during that period. In the 1800s, French architects designed wide boulevards to replace the city's narrow, crowded streets. These attractive thoroughfares still link the shopping, entertainment, and residential neighborhoods of modern Paris. To safeguard Paris's traditional architecture, developers have built skyscrapers only outside the central city.

LYON is France's second-largest city. It is home to more than 1.7 million people. Lyon has been an important urban center for more than two thousand years. Located in the middle of the Rhône River valley, the city is the hub of the French chemical industry. It is also an important center of gastronomy (culinary arts) and of textile and automobile

In Lyon diners enjoy a leisurely lunch at a streetside cafe. Lyon is a center of French culinary arts.

manufacturing. In the early 1980s, France's first high-speed train—named the Train à Grande Vitesse (TGV)—connected Lyon with Paris.

MARSEILLE has a population of more than 1.5 million. Its natural harbor on the Mediterranean has helped make it one of France's most important ports. It is also the nation's oldest city. Marseille began as a Greek colony called Massalia, founded about 2,600 years ago. In modern times, commercial ships from around the world line the busy port's docks. Colorful buildings, lively street life, and palm-lined avenues add to Marseille's attractions.

TOULOUSE AND NICE are other major cities. Toulouse has a population of more than 400,000, with more than 1 million people living in the metropolitan area. It lies along the Garonne River in south-western France. This city is the home of the French aircraft industry. Electronics, chemicals, and food processing are other industries in Toulouse. The buildings of the city's center are made of an unusual colored stone that has earned Toulouse the nickname the pink city. The Mediterranean port of Nice, home to about 350,000 people, lies at the foot of the Alps near the Italian border. During the summer, the city attracts many French and foreign tourists with its fine hotels, wide beaches, and pleasant climate. Factories in Nice produce perfumes, olive oil, soap, and cement. Nice is also the principal city of the French Riviera, a famous region of wealthy resort towns.

OTHER REGIONAL CENTERS of France developed along major river valleys or on the French coasts. For example, Bordeaux, a center of the French wine industry, lies on the Garonne River in the Aquitaine Lowlands. Strasbourg, a city on the Rhine, is the hub of France's river trade with the rest of Europe. Along the coast of the English Channel are Calais, Le Havre, and Cherbourg. These ports have commercial ties with Great Britain and serve fishing fleets, freighters, and passenger ships.

Visit www.vgsbooks.com for links to websites with information about some of France's main cities and tourist attractions.

HISTORY AND GOVERNMENT

Humans have inhabited the area that makes up modern France for nearly ten thousand years. The earliest people in this part of Europe lived in caves. They gathered plants and used stone weapons to hunt for food. These Stone Age people left cave paintings of the animals that they hunted.

About 3000 B.C., France's inhabitants began to settle in communities near rivers and seas. These people started growing food crops in these areas. In about 800 B.C., hardy warriors called Celts invaded France from the east. The Celts soon gained control of most of the European continent. Mounted on horseback, Celtic warriors defeated their enemies with iron weapons and superior numbers. In time, however, the Celtic population grew too large to survive on the conquered lands. While moving south to settle more territory, the Celts made contact with people from Greece and Rome. These two powerful civilizations were centered in southern Europe.

▶ Rome and Gaul

In the second century B.C., Rome was an expanding republic. It had a large, well-equipped army. The Romans took control of Marseille—then a Greek trading port—in 121 B.C. Roman settlers soon established other colonies in the region. They called the area Gaul.

In 58 B.C., the Roman general Julius Caesar invaded Gaul with a large army. Caesar's aim was to defeat the Celts and claim Gaul for Rome. Under the Celtic leader Vercingetorix, the Celts resisted Caesar. But they could not unify their forces to drive away his army. The war continued until 52 B.C., when the Romans defeated the Celts. The victors took Vercingetorix prisoner, and Celtic resistance to Rome ended.

The Romans soon colonized most of Gaul. Rome's engineers built roads and cities there, and Roman citizens established large farms. The Celts became successful traders and farmers and learned the Latin language of the Romans. In time, the people of Gaul adopted Christianity. It became the official Roman religion in the fourth century A.D.

A Roman-built aqueduct called the Pont du Gard spans the Gardon River in southern France. The Roman Empire ruled parts of France for five hundred years.

For several centuries, Gaul enjoyed peace and prosperity. By the middle of the fifth century A.D., however, the Roman Empire was in decline. A variety of warriors from central Europe began invading Gaul. These groups included the Visigoths, Franks, and Burgundians. Their raids weakened Rome's hold on the province.

A more serious danger threatened Gaul about 450, when Huns from Asia attacked. Their leader was the fierce warrior Attila. The Huns burned and looted farms, villages, and cities as they pushed westward. To stop them, the Frankish, Visigothic, and Burgundian armies in Gaul joined forces with Roman legions. Together they defeated Attila at the Battle of Châlons in 450. After the battle, however, Roman control of Gaul weakened further.

Rise and Fall of the Merovingians

Following Attila's downfall, the Franks gained dominance over the area of Gaul between the Rhine and Loire rivers. In 486 Clovis, the leader of the Franks, defeated a Roman army and conquered northern Gaul. He called this area Francia. Clovis united many different Frankish groups and founded the Merovingian dynasty (family of rulers). Clovis later left the Frankish religion to become a Christian. When he did, the Frankish Empire became Christian as well. The center of Christianity in western Europe was in Rome, Italy, home of the Roman Catholic Church.

Clovis died about 511. After his death, his four sons divided his empire among themselves. This division of property was customary. However, it led to countless quarrels as Clovis's heirs fought to expand their own territories. Although Francia grew to include areas in the south and east, the divided Merovingian dynasty became increasingly weak.

Advisers to the Merovingian kings controlled the realm's everyday affairs. Pépin of Herstal was the strongest of these advisers. He was a skilled military commander who brought the different states of Francia under his authority. By the time he died in 714, Pépin had established a strong kingdom. Pépin's son Charles Martel inherited the realm.

Charlemagne

Charles Martel's son established the Carolingians as a new dynasty in Francia. Charles's grandson, also named Charles, conquered the Saxons, Bavarians, and Avars. These groups all lived east of the Rhine. In southern France, the younger Charles stopped North African invaders called Moors, who had conquered Spain and Portugal.

Pépin's son Charles earned the name Martel, meaning "hammer," because of his success in battle.

Charles was an energetic ruler and a successful military campaigner. He divided his many conquests—which included much of Germany, northern Italy, and nearly all of modern France—into smaller regions. Charles appointed a loyal governor to administer each region.

In 800 Charles traveled to Rome with his army to settle a dispute between Roman officials and the pope (the leader of the Roman Catholic Church). Charles peacefully resolved the disagreement in the pope's favor. In gratitude, the pope crowned Charles emperor of western Europe. From then on, Charles was known as Charlemagne, or Charles the Great. His realm became known as the Holy Roman Empire.

Charlemagne died in 814, and his realm was divided among his

Charlemagne ruled France for forty-six years (768–814), including fourteen years as ruler of the Holy Roman Empire.

heirs. Lands west of the Rhine became the property of Charlemagne's grandson Charles the Bald. This realm, called the West Frankish Kingdom, occupied most of modern France's area.

The Carolingian rulers' power weakened during the late ninth and early tenth centuries. The Carolingians were also unable to stop the Vikings—sea raiders from northern Europe. Rich landowners built castles for protection and employed private armies. In time, these nobles became the independent rulers of the areas surrounding their castles. These wealthy landowners gradually increased their influence over the French monarchs, whom the nobles elected.

The Capetian Dynasty

The Carolingian dynasty ended in 987. In that year, the nobles chose Hugh Capet as king. Capet was a powerful duke. His lands lay between the cities of Paris and Orléans to the south. The nobles believed they had selected a man they could easily control. However, Capet arranged for his own son to inherit the French throne. This move began the Capetian dynasty in 996.

By the twelfth century, the Capetians had begun to extend their holdings. Louis VII, who reigned from 1137 to 1180, greatly expanded royal territory when he married Eleanor of Aquitaine in 1137. Eleanor was a wealthy and powerful heiress. But the couple only had daughters, and Louis wanted a son to inherit his throne. Eleanor was also unhappy in the marriage, and the couple divorced in 1152.

The vast lands of Aquitaine, however, still belonged to Eleanor. She then married Henry II, a nobleman from Normandy (a region in the north of modern-day France). When Henry II became king of England in 1154, Eleanor's property became English land. Ownership of Aquitaine caused disputes between England and France for many centuries.

Eleanor of Aquitaine owned land that included much of modern-day France. Through two marriages, her lands helped change the shape of England and France during the 1100s.

The Capetian Philip II became king of France in 1180. Philip expanded his dynasty's power through marriage and military conquests. His new possessions included the regions of Normandy and Anjou in northern France. Meanwhile, in the southern region of Provence, religious rebels angered the Catholic pope. In response, the pope launched a crusade (religious war) against them. Philip II and his successor, Louis VIII, sided with the pope and brought Provence under the French king's control.

Louis VIII's successor was Louis IX. He was a just and practical ruler. He appointed local judges to settle disputes and to hear complaints. He earned the loyalty of the French people with his fair system of government. Louis IX was also a deeply religious man. He ordered new cathedrals and religious monuments to be built in many French cities. In addition, he led religious crusaders to the Middle East and to Africa to convert Muslims there to Christianity. He died in 1270.

Philip IV reigned from 1285 to 1314. He tried to bring the Church under royal control. He also increased his authority over local officials, judges, and tax collectors. Philip called together a parliamentary (lawmaking) group known as the Estates-General in 1302. The group was made up of landowning nobles who supported Philip's reforms. The Estates-General laid the foundation for a later French legislature.

The Hundred Years' War

Philip IV's successor, Charles IV, died without an heir in 1382. Charles's cousin, Philip of Valois, inherited the throne as Philip VI. The new king became the first member of the Valois dynasty. But Philip had to compete with Edward III, then the king of England. Edward was a direct descendant of the Capetian Philip IV. He felt he was entitled to reign over France as well as England. To back up his claim, Edward invaded Normandy in 1335. This action sparked a war that would last more than one hundred years.

The Hundred Years' War began with English victories at sea and at the French port of Calais. France weakened further when the plague, a deadly disease called the Black Death, broke out in Marseille in 1348.

The last half of the fourteenth century was a time of unrest, disease, and warfare. Goods were scarce and prices rose, forcing many

THE BLACK DEATH

A deadly disease came to Europe in the 1300s through merchants and trading ships. Rats carrying plague-infected fleas arrived in European ports on ships and spread the disease. Within a few years, the plague had killed nearly one-third of the inhabitants of France. People called it the Black Death because it caused dark swollen areas on the body.

This painting from the 1800s shows the Battle of Agincourt, a decisive battle between France and England in 1415.

families into poverty and starvation. At the same time, roaming bands of soldiers robbed towns and estates throughout the kingdom. The English captured French king John II, and the French paid a huge ransom for his release. Another king, Charles VI, reigned for forty-two years while suffering from long periods of mental illness. After Henry V of England defeated French armies at Agincourt in 1415, most of France fell under English control. Charles VII succeeded Charles VI in 1422. But he was a king without a realm. He wandered from city to city while English armies controlled the countryside.

France's situation was bleak in the 1420s. Then Joan of Arc arrived at Charles's court. Joan was a peasant girl from northeastern France. Saying that angels guided her, Joan changed the course of the Hundred Years' War. Her strong devotion to the Catholic Church and to the king inspired French soldiers in the fight against the English. Joan led French forces to victory at Orléans in 1429.

This battle was the first of many English defeats. The French gradually succeeded in conquering the invading armies. However, Joan of Arc was captured in 1430 and executed by the English the following year. Eventually, Charles VII drove the English out of most of France. The Hundred Years' War ended in 1453.

Recovery and Rebirth

During the rest of the 1400s, France slowly recovered from many years of illness, deprivation, and war. Charles's successor, Louis XI, expanded his authority over French nobles. The king claimed the right to impose and to raise taxes. He also increased the kingdom's territory and created a permanent army.

By the early 1500s, France was home to a growing middle class of merchants and bankers. During the same period, an artistic movement called the Renaissance (meaning "rebirth") began in Italy and spread to France with the encouragement of King Francis I. He supported the work of skilled French artists, writers, and architects.

The early 1500s also brought the Protestant Reformation to France. This movement called for religious reform within the Catholic Church. It eventually led to a split within the Church. Protestantism became a new branch of Christianity. The Protestant Reformation spread through the teachings of the preacher John Calvin. The French Protestants, called Huguenots, quickly gained many followers.

The French monarchs and the Catholic Church saw the Huguenots as a threat to their authority. Already existing divisions within French society erupted into a religious civil war in the late sixteenth century. Many people on both sides of the conflict died. For example, in 1572 Roman Catholics attacked a crowd of Protestants in Paris, killing nearly two thousand people.

Three of Francis I's grandsons ruled in succession. They reigned under the guidance of their mother, Catherine de Médicis. In 1589 a Catholic monk assassinated Henry III, the last grandson. Henry III left no direct heir, and the Huguenot leader Henry of Navarre, a descendant of King Louis IX, took the throne. To calm Catholics who did not want a Protestant king, Henry converted to Catholicism in 1593. The first ruler of the Bourbon dynasty, Henry granted freedom of religious worship in 1598.

France became strong again under Henry. He reformed the economy and oversaw the building of new roads and canals. He reduced taxes on the common people and weakened the nobility's hold on the land.

Expansion and Excess

Despite his general popularity, Henry was assassinated by one of his subjects in 1610. Henry's young son, Louis XIII, became the new king. As a boy king and even as an adult, Louis relied on advisers to help him govern. One of his most powerful and influential advisers was a cardinal (a Catholic official) named Armand-Jean du Plessis Richelieu. Cardinal Richelieu wanted to concentrate power in the king's hands. To achieve this, the cardinal ordered the destruction or seizure of many castles and estates. Meanwhile, Louis named royal representatives to collect taxes. France's income increased as French ships and merchants established trade with North America and Africa. These early links eventually led to the founding of overseas colonies.

During Louis's reign, France joined the Netherlands and Sweden against the Habsburg dynasty. This powerful and long-standing dynasty was centered in Austria. Other European powers felt threatened by Habsburg strength, and the ongoing rivalry was one cause of the devastating Thirty Years' War. This conflict lasted from 1618 to 1648 and killed many thousands of people. France, however, gained new territory after the war and strengthened its existing borders.

Louis XIV

Louis XIII died before the war's end, in 1643. His five-year-old son, Louis XIV, inherited his crown—and a troubled nation. High taxes and poor harvests were bringing misery to the French people. A widespread rebellion called the Fronde erupted in 1648 and lasted until 1653. The royal army eventually stopped the revolt in Paris.

Louis XIV was nicknamed the Sun King. There are several theories about the nickname's origins. One theory is that, like the planets revolve around the sun, Louis believed that France's government and culture revolved around him.

Like other young kings, Louis XIV at first had help and advice from advisers. But in 1661, he took more control himself. Louis wanted to make France the world's richest and most powerful nation. New trade policies strengthened the French economy. New roads and canals linked the country's provinces. In the 1700s, French armies attacked Spain and the Netherlands to expand French territory and to place Louis's grandson on the Spanish throne.

Although most of Louis XIV's military campaigns were successful, they drained the kingdom's resources. He also earned the wrath of many when he undid the law granting religious freedom. As a result, several hundred thousand Huguenots emigrated from France to Europe and North America. These people had made up an important class of merchants and traders, and their loss weakened the French economy.

The French Revolution

After reigning for seventy-three years, Louis died in 1715. He left the throne to his five-year-old great-grandson, Louis XV. The country was then at the height of its strength. It dominated the affairs of Europe. A huge fleet of ships helped France control one of the world's largest colonial empires. French had become the international language of business, science, and diplomacy. French writers were famous throughout Europe for their new ideas of equality and civil rights.

At the same time, however, heavy taxes and poor harvests brought hardship to French laborers. Corrupt royal officials used their jobs to make themselves rich. Louis XV was unwilling to address these problems or to adapt the French economy to changing conditions. The large middle class, along with members of the nobility, demanded better government and a greater voice in running their country.

Louis XVI inherited the throne in 1774. He tried to make some reforms, but his administrators opposed them. The king's control of the government weakened as he failed to make much-needed political and financial changes. Trade competition from other European powers also weakened the nation. Violent demonstrations occurred in the countryside, and the public called for a representative assembly. In 1788 these events made Louis summon the Estates-General, which had been inactive since 1615.

The Estates-General was made up of members from the Catholic Church (the First Estate), the nobility (the Second Estate), and the middle class (the Third Estate). In 1789 the representatives of the Third Estate formed the National Assembly and wrote a new constitution. When Louis attempted to disband this new assembly, Parisians rebelled. They stormed and captured a prison in Paris called the Bastille on July 14, 1789. This act touched off the French Revolution (1789–1799). The revolution continued in Paris and spread to the provinces. The demonstrators outnumbered the king's troops.

Meanwhile, the National Assembly decreed sweeping changes in French government and society. The legislature stripped the nobility of its huge landholdings and fired corrupt judges and tax collectors.

Members of France's middle class stormed the Bastille prison in Paris on July 14, 1789, sparking the French Revolution.

Visit www.vgsbooks.com for links to websites with additional information about the French Revolution.

The assembly also took away lands belonging to the Catholic Church, angering the pope.

France became divided between forces loyal to the king and those defending the National Assembly. The nation also faced challenges from Great Britain and from the Habsburg kingdom, the leaders of which opposed the revolution. Habsburg armies invaded France in the spring of 1792. After the Habsburg forces defeated the French, another internal revolt brought down Louis and the Bourbon monarchy. Louis XVI and his wife, Queen Marie-Antoinette, were executed in 1793. The National Assembly then established the First Republic (an elected government without a king).

The First Republic and Napoléon

Forming a republic and electing a new assembly—the National Convention—were important steps for France. But they did not stop widespread unrest or foreign invasions. Some assembly members formed the Committee of Public Safety to establish order and to eliminate those who supported the monarchy. This committee executed thousands of commoners, nobles, and clergy. This period—called the Reign of Terror—lasted until 1794. Meanwhile, the new government's troops turned back the foreign armies.

In 1795 the National Convention drew up a new constitution aimed at bringing France some political stability. Nevertheless, the nation experienced four more years of unrest and violence. French people who wanted the monarchy to return opposed the new regime. They supported an energetic young general, Napoléon Bonaparte, in his bid to overthrow the republic in 1799.

Napoléon Bonaparte became the leader of France in 1799. In this painting by Jacques-Louis David, he is depicted on his horse Marengo in 1800.

Napoléon succeeded and took control of the army and the government. He was a brilliant military and political planner. Under his direction, lawyers put together a new set of laws for France. This Napoleonic Code established freedom of speech, freedom of religion, and freedom to choose a profession. The new government also overhauled the economy and replaced the royal treasury with the state-owned Bank of France.

To reestablish French military power in Europe, Napoléon successfully invaded Italy and Habsburg lands in central Europe. The rulers of these states quickly asked for peace agreements. Napoléon also settled trade and military conflicts with Great Britain and improved French relations with the Catholic Church.

These moves were all part of Napoléon's bigger aim—a French Empire that would dominate Europe. In 1804 he proclaimed himself emperor of France. Then he invaded central Europe once again. His enemies quickly drew together in an alliance to oppose him. Britain controlled the seas, blocking French ports and France's valuable trade with its colonies. Napoléon's unsuccessful attack on Russia destroyed his largest and best army. The alliance's forces drove Napoléon from Germany in 1813, and the emperor surrendered in 1814. The victorious nations placed Louis XVI's younger brother, Louis XVIII, on the throne. This action restored the Bourbon monarchy.

Napoléon's enemies exiled him to the Italian island of Elba. In March 1815, however, he returned to France at the head of a powerful French army. The allies assembled near the Belgian town of Waterloo. On June 18, 1815, they defeated Napoléon again. The emperor surrendered to the British, who sent him to Saint Helena, a remote island in the South Atlantic Ocean. Napoléon died there in 1821. For the second time, the allied nations decided that making Louis XVIII France's king was their best chance for peace. They also stationed military troops in France to maintain that peace.

The Nineteenth Century

In the early nineteenth century, France slowly recovered from Napoléon's wars and enjoyed a welcome period of peace. But its people were divided. Royalists backed the king, while Republicans supported the Chamber of Deputies (a representative assembly).

Charles X became king in 1824. He angered Republicans by establishing a stronger central government. He limited the people's right to vote and dissolved the Chamber of Deputies. Three days of riots in Paris followed these actions, forcing the king to give up his throne in 1830. Louis-Philippe of the Bourbon family became the new king.

During Louis-Philippe's reign, France rapidly became more industrialized. New factories and manufacturing methods transformed the economy. Workers moved from villages and farms to large cities. The government built railroads and schools. The monarchy, however, refused to give workers the right to vote. Only landholders could vote.

The French people's desire for their own representatives increased as the nation entered a depression (economic slowdown) in 1846. In 1848 a street demonstration in Paris turned into a widespread, violent revolt. The rebels overthrew both the constitution and the king, and Republican leaders established the Second Republic.

The Republicans adopted a new constitution and held elections. The people chose Charles Louis-Napoléon Bonaparte (Napoléon's nephew) as the Second Republic's first president. But demands for further social reforms continued, and outbreaks of urban violence were common. In 1851 the president seized total control. One year later, he proclaimed himself Emperor Napoléon III. He went on to foster further economic development. He encouraged trade with other nations and authorized building projects in the countryside and in larger cities. These changes were part of Europe's widespread industrialization.

Meanwhile, trouble brewed outside of France. Prussia (part of modern-day Germany) was building an army and attempting to form a powerful empire. To curb this threat, France declared war against Prussia in 1870. But Prussia quickly defeated the French armies, and Napoléon III surrendered himself and his forces to the Prussians. Prussia forced France to give up Alsace and Lorraine, two important northeastern provinces.

Following this defeat, French officials formed the Third Republic. They created a representative body called the National Assembly. Although disputes between Republicans and Royalists continued throughout the 1880s, further social improvements took place. Industry expanded in the late nineteenth century, and labor unions (organizations representing workers) formed. In addition, the government made schooling free and required for all children of primary school age.

During this time, France gained two important allies by signing pacts with Russia in 1894 and with Britain in 1907. The alliance of these three European powers—called the Triple Entente—was intended to balance the rising military strength of Germany. Under Prime Minister Otto von Bismarck, Germany created a three-member alliance of its own with Italy and Austria.

◉ World War I

A confrontation between the two alliances broke out in 1914. France, Great Britain, and Russia were soon at war with Germany and Austria. (Italy sided with the Entente powers.) German troops crossed Belgium into northern France, where the opposing armies fought to a standstill.

Throughout four years of fighting, neither side gained a decisive victory. But in 1918, the combined forces of Britain, the United States, and France finally drove back the German army. On November 11, 1918, Germany surrendered. Northern France had suffered widespread damage, and nearly 1.5 million French people had died.

In 1919 Germany signed the Treaty of Versailles with the war's victors. Under this agreement, Germany gave Alsace and Lorraine back to France. The treaty also demanded that Germany pay huge sums of money for damages caused by the war.

Determined to avoid another European war, French officials signed several more peace treaties. Meanwhile, the government rebuilt the French army. France also strengthened fortifications—called the Maginot Line— along the German border to stop any future attacks from the east.

France enjoyed relative stability and prosperity until 1932. In that year, a worldwide economic depression hit the French economy. Unemployment rose and factories closed, leading to strikes (work stoppages) and violence by labor union members. Many dissatisfied French people joined the Popular Front. This group was an alliance of politicians from

French soldiers fight from a trench during a 1916 battle in **World War I.**

several parties. The Popular Front won a majority of seats in the National Assembly in the 1936 elections.

Léon Blum led the new government. His administration granted many worker demands, including a shorter, forty-hour workweek. France faced an increasing military threat from Germany. Adolf Hitler had been the German leader since 1933. He was rebuilding his nation's industries to manufacture new tanks, airplanes, and warships.

France had remained closely allied with Britain in the decades after World War I. But their combined power did not stop Hitler from adding Austria to Germany in 1938 or from invading Czechoslovakia in 1939. The French and British governments tried to prevent war by allowing Hitler to keep the lands he invaded. Their strategy failed. In September 1939, German forces quickly conquered Poland, an ally of Britain and France. The Second World War had started in Europe.

A CALL TO ARMS

On June 18, 1940, Free French leader General Charles de Gaulle broadcast a message from London, England. He called on the French people to continue their fight against Germany. Part of this speech follows below.

This war is not over.... This war is a worldwide war. All the mistakes, all the delays, all the suffering, do not alter the fact that there are, in the world, all the means necessary to crush our enemies one day. Vanquished today by mechanical force, in the future we will be able to overcome by a superior mechanical force. The fate of the world depends on it.... Whatever happens, the flame of the French resistance must not be extinguished and will not be extinguished.

◉ World War II

In May 1940, German tanks invaded northern France. Paris fell within weeks. The French government asked for peace, signing a truce with Germany on June 17. When the French surrendered, Germany took direct control of two-thirds of the country. Other provinces, in the south and southeast, remained under a French administration headquartered at Vichy. The Vichy government offered no resistance to the occupying German forces.

Meanwhile, a French general named Charles de Gaulle had escaped to Great Britain. There he formed the Free French movement. He urged all French soldiers to join him in a fight against Germany's occupation. Fighters in France struggled in secret against the Germans, who built a series of defenses along the country's northwestern coast. The defenses were designed to stop any sea invasion

On August 25, 1944, General Charles de Gaulle led a victory parade through the Arc de Triomphe on the Champs-Élysées at the end of World War II.

by the Allies. The Allied forces included Great Britain, the United States, and Canada.

In 1944 Canadian, U.S., and British forces gathered in Britain and prepared to attack the European continent along the French coast. They arrived on the beaches of Normandy on June 6, 1944, liberating Paris on August 25. De Gaulle returned to the capital and organized a government. After Germany surrendered in May 1945, de Gaulle established the Fourth Republic and became its first president.

◉ Postwar Development

Once in power, de Gaulle demanded more authority. The members of the National Assembly disagreed with him, and de Gaulle resigned a year later. Vincent Auriol was elected president in 1947. René Coty succeeded him in 1953.

In the 1940s and 1950s, France focused on rebuilding its economy and improving its social welfare systems. Although France made some progress at home, postwar relations with its colonies worsened. Indochina—a large French territory in Southeast Asia—revolted in 1946. By 1954 defeats had forced France to grant self-rule to Laos, Cambodia, and Vietnam, three countries carved out of Indochina.

Charles de Gaulle fought in both World Wars I and II. He established France's Fourth Republic in 1945. After a brief retirement, de Gaulle was elected president of France and served from 1958 to 1969.

At the same time, France's North African colony of Algeria rebelled. Conflict between military and political leaders over the Algerian War (1954–1962) caused the Fourth Republic to collapse in 1958. De Gaulle left retirement to run a temporary government. A new constitution increased the authority of the president and established the Fifth Republic. Voters elected de Gaulle, head of the Gaullist Party, to a seven-year term as president.

Civil war raged in Algeria until a 1962 cease-fire. De Gaulle urged the National Assembly to recognize Algerian independence. Although the French army resisted the move, the public supported it. After Algeria became an independent nation, about one million French colonists and Algerians settled in France.

De Gaulle won another presidential term in 1965. He turned his attention to rising prices and unemployment. These problems had angered many university students. They felt that the country's economy could not provide them with good jobs and incomes. In 1968 student demonstrations in Paris led to widespread strikes and violence throughout the country. De Gaulle called for new elections, in which the Gaullists won a majority of seats in the National Assembly. But by 1969, de Gaulle had lost most voters' support. He resigned the presidency and permanently retired from politics.

De Gaulle's prime minister, Georges Pompidou, succeeded him as president after winning national elections in June 1969. The new president faced serious economic problems. The cost of oil rose sharply when oil-producing Middle Eastern countries increased their prices. France, which imported most of its petroleum, had to adjust to a critical shortage of fuel. Unemployment was still rising, as was inflation (rapidly rising prices of goods). Pompidou died in 1974, leaving these problems unsolved.

Ongoing Challenges

Valéry Giscard d'Estaing was France's next president. He promised to resolve disputes among the French leaders. His prime minister, Raymond Barre, was a skillful economic planner. But Barre, like other leaders, struggled with the problems of the French economy.

In 1981 French voters chose François Mitterand to succeed Giscard as president. Mitterand was a member of the French Socialist Party. Mitterand nationalized (placed under state control) banks and large industries. He also raised taxes to pay for increased benefits such as health care.

Support for Mitterand's party dropped in the late 1980s. In the early 1990s, unemployment and inflation continued to plague France.

In 1993 France became one of the founding members of the European Union (EU). This organization of European nations supports cooperation among its members in trade, politics, and economics.

Jacques Chirac

Amid these changes, Mitterand's administration still struggled with economic issues. These problems led to the Socialist Party's defeat in the 1995 presidential election. Jacques Chirac, the mayor of Paris, became president.

Chirac promised economic reform. But trade unions and political opponents in the legislature blocked many of his efforts. Chirac's problems mounted in 1997 when legislative elections brought defeat for his party. Socialist Party leader Lionel Jospin became the new prime minister, forcing President Chirac into an uneasy coalition with one of his political opponents.

Developments and Demonstrations

Another economic change soon followed, as France adopted the EU's common currency, the euro. It officially replaced the French franc in 2002. Also in 2002, voters reelected Chirac president. But he promptly faced challenges. In October, workers launched massive strikes. They were protesting the government's plans to privatize (move from government control to private owners) utility companies. The following year brought a disagreement between France and the United States, when France opposed the 2003 U.S. invasion of Iraq.

More internal unrest followed in 2005. Further strikes erupted, this time protesting government plans to lengthen the workweek and to cut health and retirement benefits. The same year, two fires broke out in overcrowded, rundown apartment buildings in Paris, killing forty-one people. These buildings were home to immigrant families who were waiting—sometimes for years—for the government to assign them permanent housing. A few months later, two immigrant youths died. Reports that police had been chasing them caused an outcry, and riots broke out in poor neighborhoods and immigrant communities. The violence quickly spread beyond Paris. It lasted for almost three weeks, and nearly three thousand people were arrested.

February through April of 2006 saw huge protests over proposed changes to employment law. These laws aimed to create new jobs, but they also gave employers more freedom to fire young employees. In April, in response to the widespread marches, protests, and riots, Chirac scrapped the laws.

Nicolas Sarkozy became president in the spring of 2007. Like earlier presidents, he found his time in office soon marred by violence. Protests and strikes broke out in November of 2007 over proposed retirement benefit cuts. That same month, the deaths of two immigrant youths—once again in an incident linked with the French police—sparked widespread riots.

French president Nicolas Sarkozy *(right)* and his wife, Carla Bruni-Sarkozy, *(second from right)* **are pictured with U.S. president Barack Obama and his wife, Michelle, in April 2009 during a summit in Strasbourg for the North Atlantic Treaty Organization (NATO).**

In 2010 Sarkozy's government was still working to solve the nation's economic and social problems. New laws aimed to stimulate the sluggish economy, while other measures focused on addressing tensions and divisions in French society.

Government

French citizens who are eighteen years old and older are eligible to vote. They elect a president every five years. This president can serve an unlimited number of terms. According to the constitution of the Fifth Republic (adopted in 1958), the president has the power to call new elections and to propose treaties and constitutional amendments. He or she may also take control of the government during national emergencies.

The president selects the country's prime minister, who is usually a political ally of the president. The prime minister directs the Council of Ministers, which is comprised of the heads of government ministries.

The country's federal legislature is made up of the National Assembly and the Senate. Voters of each district elect their own delegates to the National Assembly, which has 577 members. These delegates serve five-year-terms. The Senate is a 321-member advisory body. Regional and city representatives elect senators.

France's judicial system is based on the nineteenth-century Napoleonic Code. Local courts, called tribunals, exist in each region. The Court of Assize hears all major criminal cases, and its judges are elected. France's highest court, the Court of Cassation, can review cases and return them to any of the lower courts. The president appoints its judges.

France has ninety-six local administrative units, called departments, including the two departments of the island of Corsica. The national government appoints a commissioner to govern each department. In addition, each department's residents elect a local council. The smallest administrative units in France are communes—cities, towns, and rural communities. Each commune has a council and a mayor.

CHANGING FRANCE

Following his election, Nicolas Sarkozy chose a diverse cabinet (group of advisers). It included seven women, one of whom was Justice Minister Rachida Dati. Dati was the first woman of North African descent to serve in the French cabinet. (Her parents are immigrants from Morocco and Algeria.)

THE PEOPLE

France is home to a total of 62.6 million people (including those in its overseas departments). The European portion of France (not counting its overseas territories) has about 60.2 million residents. The population is growing at a rate of about 0.4 percent. If it continues at this rate, the nation will have an estimated 70 million people by the year 2050.

More than three-quarters of French residents live in urban areas. The overall population density of France is about 295 people per square mile (114 people per sq. km). In comparison, France's neighbor Belgium has 917 residents per square mile (354 per sq. km), while Spain is home to 241 people per square mile (93 per sq. km). However, people are not spread throughout France evenly. Urban areas dominate the country's northern half, which has a higher population density than southern France has. In the north, many French workers hold jobs in industry and in the service sector. South of the Loire River, more people are employed in agriculture and live on farms and in small villages.

Ethnic Identity

Most French people have a mixed European heritage. This mixing dates back to France's very early history, when the Celts intermarried with Roman and Germanic settlers. Over the centuries, various regions of France also absorbed other ethnic groups. For example, Viking invaders from Norway and Denmark left descendants in Normandy. Northeastern France, including Alsace, is home to many people of German background. The Bretons of the Brittany Peninsula in northwestern France have maintained their distinctive Celtic language, local cuisine, and traditional clothing. The Basques of southwestern France also have their own language, and many have joined with Spanish Basques in demanding a separate nation.

During the twentieth century, France's ethnic landscape broadened again. A shortage of workers attracted thousands of immigrants to France from southern Europe, as well as from Africa. Some African immigrants came from former French territories in western and central

France's population includes immigrants from its former African territories.

Africa, such as Mali (which won independence in 1960). And after Algeria won its independence in 1962, nearly one million French colonists and Algerians moved to France. Many other North Africans have also arrived, either as war refugees or as laborers seeking work on farms and in factories. Immigration from North Africa has continued at a high pace into the twenty-first century. At times, competition for jobs and clashes in culture have caused friction between people of North African descent and ethnically French people in Marseille and in other large urban areas.

◉ Health

France has a comprehensive social-security system that provides health insurance and other benefits for nearly all citizens—about 99 percent of the nation's people. The plan pays for medicine, medical treatment, and hospitalization. French citizens contribute to the health-care system through their taxes, and employers also help pay for the health coverage of their workers. Some of these funds go to public hospitals, which make up about 65 percent of all the nation's hospitals. Some people use public facilities, as well as pay extra to use private hospitals. Studies show that public and private institutions are about equal in the quality of their care. However, doctors and hospitals are concentrated in the nation's cities, and care can be harder to reach in parts of rural France.

Overall, French health statistics reflect this strong system. The average life expectancy at birth is 81 years (78 years for men, and 84 for women). The birthrate in 2009—13 births per 1,000 people—is among the highest in Western Europe. The number of babies who die within their first year is 3.6 per 1,000, while Europe's overall average is 6 per 1,000.

France and its people do face health problems and challenges, however. Cancer and cardiovascular disease are both leading causes of death among the French. The spread of human immunodeficiency virus (HIV) and acquired immunodeficiency syndrome (AIDS) is also a concern among doctors and government officials. French physicians were among the first to isolate and identify HIV, which causes AIDS. The Pasteur Institute in Paris remains a leading center for the treatment of the disease. France's rate of infection is about 0.4 percent of the population—one of the highest in Western Europe. An estimated 140,000 or more people in France are living with HIV/AIDS.

◉ Education

France has a comprehensive public education system. French nursery schools are free and available to children between the ages of two and six. Compulsory (required by law), free public education begins at the age of six and lasts through the age of sixteen. The nation boasts about a 99 percent enrollment rate for students in this age range.

At six years old, French students enroll in elementary school. When they reach eleven, students enter a *collège* for four more years of schooling in a nationwide curriculum. The next step in a French pupil's education is the *lycée*. The lycée is a three-year high school.

Students in Le Havre work at their desks. Free education is available to all French children.

Students take the baccalauréat exam. Those who pass the test will be eligible to receive higher education at universities or professional schools.

(Students are not legally required to complete their lycée years.) It prepares students either for universities or for vocational and technical training in specific fields. Students who plan to enter the higher-education system must first pass an examination called the *baccalauréat*. More than 15 percent of all candidates fail this difficult test.

In addition to the public school system, France has private schools. About 15 to 20 percent of French students attend private institutions. The Roman Catholic Church runs most of these schools.

A total of about 2.25 million students attend French universities or the more specialized *grandes écoles*. Universities provide education in a wide variety of subjects. A famous institution in this system is the University of Paris, which dates back to the 1100s. The grandes écoles, on the other hand, offer more targeted instruction in various professional fields. For example, the prestigious École Normale Supérieure in Paris prepares students for jobs as professors or government officials. Other grandes écoles focus on subjects such as engineering, literature, or business.

At every level of schooling, classes are conducted in French.

STAR PUPILS

The École Normale Supérieure in Paris has a reputation as one of France's very best schools. Its former students include scientist Louis Pasteur, writer and philosopher Jean-Paul Sartre, and more than ten winners of the Nobel Prize.

Overall, France has a national literacy rate (the number of adults who can read and write a basic sentence) of about 99 percent.

◑ Languages

French—the official language of France—originally developed from the Latin tongue. Latin was once spoken throughout the Roman Empire. The Celts adopted it and introduced their own words, as well as their own pronunciation. Later, the Franks and related Germanic peoples also influenced early forms of French.

The two primary Old French dialects were named for words meaning "yes"—*oeil* in the north and *oc* in the south.

In about A.D. 1000, two main dialects of Old French arose—*langue d'oeil* in the north and *langue d'oc* in the south. Contact with various civilizations brought words from Greek, Spanish, and Italian into Old French. Gradually, the language spoken around the city of Paris became the dominant form. Writers, diplomats, businesspeople, and members of the royal court all used this Parisian brand of French.

Although langue d'oc became the less commonly used French dialect (language subgroup), it does survive in modern times as Provençal. This tongue is the second language of many people in southern France. Other languages in France include Breton (a Celtic language spoken in

Signs in French direct visitors to specific spots in the town of Chinon in northwestern France.

Brittany) and Alsatian (a German dialect used in Alsace). The Basque language has survived in southwestern France, and some people living in and around the French Pyrenees speak French Catalan.

City Life and Country Life

By far, most of France's people live in cities or large towns. More than 75 percent of the population is urban, and 25 percent of French residents live in cities of at least 750,000 people. Most French city dwellers live in apartment buildings, but those who live on the outskirts of larger cities or in smaller cities may have houses. They have jobs in offices, shops, schools, factories, and a variety of other workplaces. Many Parisians work for the government. In their free time, urban French people have a wide variety of options open to them for recreation. They might see films, go to the theater, attend concerts, dine out at fine restaurants, or visit with friends at cafés.

For the 25 percent of people who live in the French countryside or in small villages, life moves at a slower pace. In many ways, country life in France has changed little over the centuries. While modern technology has made many daily tasks easier and more convenient, life generally centers on farming and the seasons. The typical French village has a small main street with shops including butchers and bakeries. Rural families usually live in small houses in the village or in farmhouses surrounded by their fields.

Dairy farmers stand outside their barn in France. Many rural families rely on farming and agriculture to make a living.

A family walks through an outdoor market in Paris. Although big grocery stores are common in France, many people still shop at traditional markets.

▶ Women and Families

Many French women work outside the home. In addition, more and more women are achieving higher professional positions and winning political office. In general, discrimination and prejudice based on gender are not major problems. However, female employees do receive lower pay than their male counterparts.

The family has long been a cornerstone of French society, and families are still close-knit units in modern France. Most ethnically European families in the country are small, with only one or two children. Many French families of North African descent have four or more children. Other social norms are also changing. In the twenty-first century, the nation has also seen a rising number of single-parent families and children born outside of marriage.

More than 60 percent of French women hold jobs outside the home.

Visit www.vgsbooks.com for links to websites with additional information about France's education, health, and other demographic statistics.

CULTURAL LIFE

France's history has given it a long-standing cultural legacy. In modern times, its diverse population has added depth and variety to the country's culture. Woven together, these different elements form a rich cultural tapestry.

▶ Religion

Throughout most of French history, the Roman Catholic Church has been closely tied to French education and family life. France has not had an official state religion since 1905. In modern France, an estimated 81 percent of citizens identify themselves as Roman Catholics. Among this number, however, are many people who rarely or never attend church.

Other Christian residents of France include Protestants, who make up about 1.6 percent of French people. Most of them belong to the Reformed (Calvinist) Church. Lutherans and Baptists are other important Protestant sects. Members of the Russian, Greek, and

Armenian Orthodox churches comprise approximately 0.4 percent of the population.

The second-largest religion in France is Islam. Most of the North Africans who have immigrated to France follow this faith, and Muslims make up an estimated 8 percent of French residents. Hundreds of mosques (Islamic places of worship) sit alongside the nation's many Christian churches.

Large Jewish communities exist in Paris and Marseille, and Jews make up about 1.3 percent of the population. In addition, about 0.7 percent of French residents are Buddhists. The remaining 7 percent of French people follow other religions or none at all.

Holidays and Festivals

The historical predominance of Christianity in France means that most residents observe many Christian holidays. Christmas, on December 25, is one of the most important of these celebrations.

CHURCH AND STATE

Religion has been an issue of tension and debate in modern France. For example, controversy surrounded a 2004 law that banned "wearing of conspicuous religious symbols in public schools." These symbols include the head scarves worn by many Muslim women and girls. Supporters of the law argued that it would discourage discrimination against people based on their religions, while opponents said that it violated the right of religious freedom.

Christian families attend midnight church services on Christmas Eve and come home to *le réveillon*, a late-night meal of many courses. Before bed, children in southern France leave their shoes out, hoping they will be filled with candy, nuts, and other gifts from Père Nöel (Father Christmas). Easter, which falls in the spring, is an even more important celebration in the church year. French Christians observe the holiday by going to church and enjoying a festive meal. Children hunt for colored eggs and receive sweet treats of chocolate bells, a traditional Easter candy in France.

For the country's Muslim population, the holy month of Ramadan is the most sacred time of the year. The dates of Ramadan change every year, because the lunar (moon-based) calendar determines these dates. Muslims observe Ramadan by fasting, or eating nothing, between sunrise and sunset. The month is a time for

Muslims pray outside the Grande Mosquée de Paris on Eid al-Fitr, the final day of Ramadan. The Grande Mosquée is the largest mosque in France and the second largest mosque in all of Europe.

During Bastille Day festivities, a military parade marches down the Champs-Élysées in Paris. Other events include music, fireworks, and air shows.

prayer, services at mosques, and quiet contemplation. However, it is also a festive time. After dark, a meal called the *iftar* breaks each day's fast, and many friends and families meet in the evening to share this meal together. The end of Ramadan is celebrated with a magnificent feast and festival called Eid al-Fitr. Another important Islamic holiday is Eid al-Adha. The festival commemorates a story in the Quran (Islam's holy book). It takes place at the time of the annual hajj, a pilgrimage to the Islamic holy city of Mecca, Saudi Arabia.

The French also celebrate a number of secular (nonreligious) holidays. The biggest of these celebrations is Bastille Day, on July 14. It commemorates the 1789 storming of the Bastille prison, viewed as the symbolic birth of modern France. French cities mark the holiday with fireworks, parades, music, and general merriment. Other national holidays honor France's role in the world wars. November 11 marks the anniversary of the 1918 armistice ending World War I, and May 8 commemorates the 1945 victory of the Allied powers in World War II. In addition to these national holidays, many towns and villages hold local festivals, often during summer.

Literature

Literature has long had an important place in French culture. France's earliest poets were wandering minstrels. They composed and performed songs in castles and towns. Narrative poems of noble deeds, such as *The Song of Roland*, entertained French rulers and their courts. In the 1400s and 1500s, literary and scholarly works of the French Renaissance took ideas from ancient Greek and Roman writers. François Rabelais's five-part story *Gargantua and Pantagruel* made fun of religious and social institutions. Michel de Montaigne described his life and thoughts in essay form.

Molière *(left)* and Victor Hugo *(right)* are two of France's great writers.

The seventeenth century was a golden age of poetry and drama in France. The dramatists Pierre Corneille and Jean Racine wrote tragedies based on ancient Greek and Roman myths. The playwright Molière published comedies that criticized and made fun of the French upper class. René Descartes and Blaise Pascal were two important philosophers who wrote during this era.

During the eighteenth century, French writers believed that the use of reason could solve social and philosophical problems. In novels and essays, Voltaire and Jean-Jacques Rousseau wrote in favor of civil rights for all citizens. The *Encyclopédie* of Denis Diderot classified and explained knowledge and discoveries in many different scientific fields.

After the French Revolution, Victor Hugo wrote *The Hunchback of Notre Dame* and *Les Misérables*. These two great works of historical fiction are set in Paris. Other French writers of the 1800s wrote novels based on modern French life. Honoré de Balzac and Gustave Flaubert favored realistic descriptions of French society. Émile Zola's series of novels portrays the members of a large family and the challenges they encounter. Many talented French poets also gained prominence in the late 1800s. They included Charles Baudelaire, Paul Verlaine, Stéphane Mallarmé, and Arthur Rimbaud.

Leading writers of the early twentieth century, such as André Gide and Paul Claudel, broke free of traditional literary styles. Marcel Proust's *Remembrance of Things Past* is a seven-part autobiographical work containing deep insights into psychology and society. Exploration of the mind also fascinated writers including Louis Aragon and André Breton in the 1920s and 1930s.

After World War II, writers found new material in questions about individual freedom, existence, and morality. Jean-Paul Sartre and Simone de Beauvoir were the leading thinkers of this new philosophy, called existentialism. Sidonie-Gabrielle Colette wrote a large number

Marguerite Duras

of novels during the first half of the twentieth century. Albert Camus was a French writer from Algeria. He questioned modern government, religion, and society in his novels, plays, and essays. Other modern French novelists have included Alain Robbe-Grillet, Marguerite Duras, and Claude Simon. They have all experimented with traditional forms of the novel.

Contemporary writers in France include Gao Xingjian, who was born in China and has been a French citizen since 1997. A playwright, novelist, and screenwriter, he won the Nobel Prize in Literature in 2000. French author J. M. G. Le Clézio, who writes novels, short stories, and essays, won the prize in 2008. Other current authors include Ann Scott, who writes fiction exploring the lives of alienated and frustrated youths. Her 2000 novel, *Superstars*, won her a dedicated following in France. Young author Romain Sardou writes historical fiction as well as crime thrillers and science fiction.

French writers have won sixteen Nobel Prizes in Literature, including the first one ever awarded. Sully Prudhomme won this prize in 1901.

Art and Architecture

Painting in France flourished during the Renaissance. During that period, wealthy French aristocrats invited Italian artists to beautify castles and palaces. Italian painting also influenced the seventeenth-century French artists Georges de La Tour and Nicolas Poussin. In the eighteenth century, painters used elaborate detail to depict domestic scenes and mythological subjects for their wealthy clients. In the early nineteenth century, the artists Eugène Delacroix and Jacques-Louis David often used huge canvases to portray historic events.

Paris became an international center of painting in the late 1800s, when French artists brought impressionism to the capital. This method of painting allowed artists to experiment with light and color on their canvases. Among the most famous French impressionists were Edouard Manet, Claude Monet, Pierre-Auguste Renoir, and Paul Cézanne. Several twentieth-century artistic movements, such as cubism, Dadaism, and surrealism, began in Paris. These new forms left the rules of conventional

In 1981 Jean Nouvel designed the Arab World Institute, which sits on the Seine's Left Bank in Paris. The building features a metallic screen made up of 240 moving geometric patterns. These squares *(inset)*, which operate like a camera's shutter, open and close mechanically to allow in more or less light.

painting behind. They focused instead on abstract shapes, playful imagery, and unusual techniques.

Contemporary French artists continue to build on artistic traditions and to explore their own styles. Christian Boltanski creates sculptures, paintings, and photographs. His works tend to be serious and often focus on death. Many draw on French and world history. Tounille is a painter whose mostly abstract works are full of bold colors and shapes. Danièle Jaquillard creates vividly colored abstract paintings. She also takes photographs in a variety of styles.

Architecture is another aspect of France's visual arts. French architects pioneered many building techniques in the nineteenth and twentieth centuries. For example, cast iron was first used in the construction of the Eiffel Tower, which began as a temporary structure for the Paris World's Fair of 1889. The tower stands near the banks of the Seine in Paris. Le Corbusier was a twentieth-century pioneer in the design of both private and public buildings. Jean Nouvel is an award-winning contemporary architect. His buildings are located around Europe and beyond and include the Guthrie Theater in Minneapolis, Minnesota.

Music

One of France's early musical forms was the *chanson de geste*. This type of long narrative song appeared between the eleventh and the thirteenth centuries. Singer-poets called troubadours were also part of early French music from the 1100s until about 1300. Music for religious ceremonies dominated the work of French composers during the Renaissance. Later, during the reign of Louis XIV, Jean-Baptiste Lully combined dance, drama, and music into large-scale productions. These spectacles developed into a French style of opera, which became an important musical form. In the 1700s, Jean-Philippe Rameau added extravagant staging to his operas.

The opera and the symphony influenced French musicians during the nineteenth century. Hector Berlioz, the creator of *Symphonie Fantastique*, was one of Europe's leading composers. Other important writers of symphonies were Camille Saint-Saëns and Gabriel Fauré. Georges Bizet composed the music for *Carmen*, which remains one of the world's most popular operas.

Many French musicians, influenced by impressionism, tried to create new styles and forms of music. Claude Debussy's piano works caused a sensation with their unusual scales and harmonies. Maurice Ravel, who often drew upon musical forms from earlier centuries, paved the way for new composing techniques that arose in the 1920s and 1930s.

France also has a rich tradition of folk and popular music. The singers Édith Piaf and Maurice Chevalier achieved great popularity after World War II. Serge Gainsbourg, who started as a jazz pianist in Parisian nightclubs, was one of France's biggest musical stars until his death in 1995. Other recent French musicians, such as Pierre Boulez, have created new styles of electronic music using modern technology.

Édith Piaf, photographed here in 1936, is one of France's most famous and beloved singers. Her signature song, "La Vie en Rose," was written in 1945.

Hip-hop artists *(left to right)* Disiz la Peste, Diams, and Soprano perform during the 2006 French music awards.

In addition to pop and rock music, rap and especially hip-hop are popular modern forms in France. Some French hip-hop stars, such as the band IAM and the solo artists MC Solaar and Sheryo, have gained followings at home as well as in other countries.

Many popular musicians in modern France draw on diverse ethnic influences and backgrounds, including Caribbean and North African styles. One genre that has been growing in popularity is *raï*, a form of Algerian folk music usually sung in Arabic. Modern raï artists blend traditional folk themes with contemporary styles such as pop, rock, and hip-hop. Raï music's lyrics often include political, religious, or historical messages. It is especially popular among France's Muslims.

Performing Arts and Film

The people of France produce and enjoy many forms of performing arts. Dance—from folk dance to ballet to modern choreography—thrives. In addition, theater has long been a popular form of French art and entertainment, and the nation has produced many great playwrights. Paris is home to the country's national theater, which dates back to the 1600s. The capital city also holds the national ballet and opera house.

French cinema is famous around the globe. The country was home to one of the world's first film industries, producing early movies around the end of the 1800s. Ever since these beginnings, France has been a center of filmmaking. The annual Cannes Film Festival is one of the most prestigious events in the world of cinema, drawing huge international stars. French filmmakers and actors such as Jean-Luc Godard and Juliette Binoche have had great success at home and beyond.

▶ Food

French cooking has been world-renowned for centuries. Yet an ordinary meal prepared in a French home is likely to be simple. The main meal of the day may have several courses. Soup or an appetizer begins the meal. A main course of meat or fish is next and may come with potatoes, rice, or fresh vegetables. A garden salad follows the main course. A crusty loaf of French bread, called a baguette, accompanies the meal. Several varieties of cheese, each from a different region of the country, are often served before dessert. Finally, diners might enjoy sweet treats such as pastries, crepes (very thin pancakes), or fruit.

CHOCOLATE MOUSSE

This rich, sweet dessert is a French classic.

1 envelope unsweetened gelatin powder

¼ cup cold water

½ cup milk

2 squares unsweetened baking chocolate

1 square semisweet baking chocolate

½ cup sugar

2 cups heavy cream

additional whipped cream and/ or grated chocolate (optional)

1. In a medium bowl, combine gelatin with water. Set aside.
2. In a medium saucepan, combine milk and the 3 chocolate squares. Over low heat, stir until the chocolate melts completely. Add the sugar. Stir until it dissolves completely.
3. Place the heavy cream in a medium bowl. Use an electric mixer to beat the cream until it thickens and forms soft peaks.
4. Pour the chocolate mixture into a large mixing bowl. Use a spoon to combine the gelatin mixture with the chocolate.
5. Use a rubber scraper to fold one-third of the cream into the chocolate. Then fold in the remaining beaten cream.
6. Pour into a serving bowl or into individual serving dishes and cover with plastic wrap.
7. Chill in the refrigerator for at least 2 hours. If desired, decorate with whipped cream and/or grated sweet chocolate before serving.

Serves 4.

Appetizers are an important part of the traditional French menu. Pâté de foie gras is a delicate spread made from goose liver. Escargot are snails from Burgundy cooked in butter, parsley, and garlic. Truffles—black mushrooms that specially trained pigs dig up—are a rare and expensive delicacy.

Cooks around France prepare many regional specialties. These dishes include cassoulet, a stew of white beans, pork, chicken, and sausage in tomato sauce from the region of Toulouse. Bouillabaisse is a thick fish soup from Marseille, and Corsican specialties include a chestnut soup made with goat's milk. Alsatian cooks make choucroute garnie with various meats and sauerkraut. Seafood—including oysters, mussels, shrimp, crab, and lobster—is popular all along the French coast. Other dishes around France are associated with certain holidays. For example, a traditional Christmas dessert is the *bûche de Nöel*, a rich, log-shaped cake filled with chocolate or chestnut-flavored cream.

French wines accompany all courses of a traditional main meal. Many of the red wines from Bordeaux and Burgundy are world famous. White wines from the Loire Valley and rosé wines from Anjou often accompany fish courses. A small region east of Paris produces excellent champagne for festive occasions and for family celebrations.

Sports

France's varied terrain offers a wide range of sports and leisure activities. For instance, downhill and cross-country skiing are both popular in the mountains. In the summer, many French people hike or climb in the Alps, the Pyrenees, or the Massif Central. Also in summer, swimmers and sunbathers crowd the long seacoasts along the Mediterranean and the Atlantic Ocean.

In parks and town squares throughout the country, men play the game of *pétanque* year-round. In pétanque, two teams compete in throwing small metal balls, aiming to land closest to an even smaller wooden ball at a distance. Tennis, fishing, handball, and ice-skating are other popular activities.

France's low-lying countryside is ideal for bicyclists. Many people use bicycles to travel short distances. Bicycle racing is one of the country's favorite sports. The Tour de France, the world's most famous bicycle race, is a grueling, three-week test of cyclists' strength and endurance. It draws millions of

SPORTS CENTER

France has hosted the Olympic Games five times. It welcomed the Summer Games in 1900 and 1924 and the Winter Games in 1924, 1968, and 1992. French Olympic athletes excel in cycling, fencing, and alpine skiing.

Fans cheer on cyclists climbing a mountain road during the Tour de France in 2009.

viewers. Thousands line the racecourse, enjoying picnics and cheering for their favorite teams and athletes. Others watch the competition on televisions all around the globe.

Soccer—called football in France—remains the country's most popular team sport by far. Most cities and towns have local teams, and many French children play the game from a young age. France's national team, nicknamed Les Bleus (the Blues), has competed in many international tournaments. The team has played in the World Cup twelve times. This large tournament brings together teams from all over the world every four years. Les Bleus won the World Cup in 1998, and in 2006, they made it to the finals but lost to Italy. Other team sports that the French enjoy include rugby, volleyball, and basketball.

> For links to more information about the Tour de France, visit www.vgsbooks.com.

THE ECONOMY

Once a largely agricultural nation, France rapidly industrialized in the early twentieth century. The world wars, however, stopped the nation's economic expansion. After World War II ended in 1945, government programs rebuilt important industries, constructed housing, and improved services. The state took control of banks and the transportation system.

France experienced rapid growth until the late 1970s, when greater overseas competition and higher energy costs slowed the economy. To survive, many small family-owned companies merged into larger firms. Heavy industries, such as steel and automobile making, cut costs by streamlining production. But both of these trends caused unemployment to rise. While the economy rebounded somewhat and grew in the late 1990s, ongoing unemployment and inflation have remained problems in the twenty-first century.

Despite these challenges, most French people enjoy a high standard of living compared to people in most of the world. The nation's gross

national income (GNI) per person is $34,400. GNI is a measure of how much money people in different nations earn. The French average is higher than the European average of $25,550. By comparison, the average GNI in Asia is $6,020. In the United States, it is $46,970.

▶ Services and Trade

France's service industry is by far the largest area of its economy. It accounts for about 75 percent of the country's gross domestic product. (Abbreviated as GDP, gross domestic product is a measure of the total annual value of goods and services produced by a nation's workers.) Activities in the service sector include government work, banking, insurance, health care, retail sales, tourism, and other jobs that supply services rather than produce goods. This large sector also employs approximately 74 percent of all the nation's workers.

Tourism is a major part of the nation's service sector and a very valuable source of foreign income. More than 75 million visitors from

Tourists on a beach in Cannes enjoy the sun, sand, and surf along the country's famous Riviera coastline.

all over the world vacation in France each year. Tourism adds more than $40 million to the country's economy annually. Most tourists come from the United Kingdom, Ireland, and Germany. Principal destinations include the city of Paris, the Mediterranean and Atlantic coasts, and the river valleys, especially the Loire Valley. Nature reserves in the Pyrenees and in the Massif Central attract hikers, climbers, and campers. The French Riviera, on the Mediterranean coast, has long been a favorite spot for visitors. Many resorts also lie along the Atlantic coast of Aquitaine in southwestern France.

Foreign trade is another important aspect of the French economy. France imports much of the fuel it needs for domestic and industrial use. Other major imports include electric equipment, manufactured foods, and chemicals. The nation exports automobiles, textiles, aircraft, and agricultural products. France's most important trading partners are fellow European Union members—primarily Germany, Italy, Belgium, Spain, and the United Kingdom. More than 60 percent of French exports go to other EU countries. France's main trading partner outside the EU is the United States.

Manufacturing and Industry

With careful planning and extensive foreign aid, France rebuilt many damaged and destroyed factories after World War II. Governmental control of major industries also helped the nation supply essential products during the postwar era. In modern France, manufacturing, industry, and mining account for about 22.5 percent of the nation's

GDP. This sector employs about 22.5 percent of French workers. France's major industries make vehicles, steel, and chemicals.

The French automobile industry is among the top ten largest in the world. Auto plants in Paris, Rennes, and other French cities produce more than three million cars each year for export and for domestic sale. Major automakers include Renault and Peugeot. Aircraft and aerospace equipment are also leading industries, and their largest French center is in Toulouse.

The country's iron and steel factories are concentrated in eastern and northern France. Much of the iron ore necessary for the production of steel is mined in Lorraine. Steelworks on the Mediterranean coast and in Dunkerque contribute to the country's annual output of more than 21 million tons (19 million metric tons) of steel.

Textiles, a traditional French industry, provide a livelihood for many workers. Shops in regional centers weave wool, cotton, silk, and synthetic fibers into cloth. Factories in the Paris region supply finished clothing as part of France's prominent fashion industry.

Agriculture

Agriculture comprises only about 2.5 percent of France's present-day GDP. It employs approximately 3.5 percent of the country's workforce. Nevertheless, it remains an important facet of the French economy.

French farmers benefit from a mild climate, fertile soil, and the economic support of the French government. Small farms once dominated French agriculture, but many family farms have been combined into larger estates. Roughly one-third of the land in France is under cultivation.

Many French farmers plant grain crops. In fact, France produces more grain than any other European nation. The primary French grain crops are wheat, corn, and barley. These grains grow well in northern and central France. Sugar beets are also an important crop, ranking second only to wheat in volume. Other vegetable crops include potatoes, carrots, tomatoes, and lettuce. Fruit orchards, olives, and sunflowers thrive in southern France's dry climate.

Grapes also flourish in France. Many of them go into making the fine French wines that are famous throughout the world. Wine grapes grown in Bordeaux, the Loire Valley, Burgundy, and the Rhône Valley thrive in the dry, well-drained soils of these regions.

In addition to crops, France also earns agricultural income from meat and dairy production. The nation's grasslands and hillsides support more than 19 million cattle, close to 15 million pigs, and nearly 9 million sheep. The country is a leading producer of milk and cheese, which come mainly from farms in the mountainous areas of the east and south, and also from Normandy. Northern and western France offer good pastures for horses. French farmers also raise millions of chickens, ducks, and turkeys.

Fishing and Forestry

France's fishing industry is small but continues a long tradition. The nation's principal fishing ports, including Boulogne-sur-Mer and Lorient, lie along the Normandy and Brittany coasts. Thousands of fishing boats ply coastal waters, as well as more distant areas in the North Atlantic Ocean. They pull in catches of tuna, herring, whiting, sardines, and a variety of shellfish.

In addition, oyster farms abound in the regions of Charente and Les Landes (in southwestern France). Oyster farmers use salty lagoons to raise these shellfish for sale at home and abroad. France is also home to commercial farms raising

These trays hold shellfish that are farmed for sale. Farmed shellfish are good for the environment too, because the shellfish clean the water in which they live.

freshwater fish such as trout. The French fishing industry brings in an annual catch of more than 900,000 tons (816,466 metric tons).

France's forests also provide the nation with some income. Approximately one-fourth of French land is wooded. The heaviest forest cover lies in the mountains and along the Mediterranean coast. These forests produce wood for use as fuel, building material, and other purposes.

Mining and Energy

French supplies of coal once provided most of the country's fuel for homes and industries. But the coal-mining regions of northern France suffered when other fuels, such as oil, began to provide heat and electricity. Although modern France has petroleum refineries, it must import most of its crude oil from the Middle East, from Africa, and from fellow European nations. Oil fields in Les Landes and natural gas from the Pyrenees meet some of the country's energy needs.

France has been a leading producer of bauxite since the discovery of this mineral near the French town of Les Baux-de-Provence in the nineteenth century. Bauxite is an important component of aluminum production. Alsace and Lorraine provide potash and phosphates, which are refined into agricultural fertilizers. Salt, taken from mines and evaporated from seawater in factories along the coast, is used in food processing. French mines also produce zinc, lead, iron ore, and gold.

France is home to the world's first tidal power plant, built in 1967 on the Rance River in Brittany. It uses the movement of very high tides near the port of Saint-Malo to generate electric power.

The French government supports an extensive nuclear power program, which provides about 80 percent of the nation's electricity. More than fifty reactors are in operation, and plans exist for building more. In addition, hydroelectric dams and power plants use the power of France's rushing rivers to create electricity.

Transportation

France has one of Europe's most extensive and modern road networks. More than 6,000 miles (9,656 km) of expressways connect the principal cities. Smaller highways and roads also connect cities, towns, and villages. More than 28 million cars, plus many trucks, buses, scooters, and motorcycles, travel the nation's roads.

Workers have blasted tunnels through mountains to build highways in the Alps near the Italian border. The Eurotunnel—an underwater tunnel linking France and England—opened in 1994. Passing under the

RIDING (UNDER) THE WAVES

The Eurotunnel took six years to build (1988–1994) and cost $21 billion. It is 31 miles (50 km) long, and at its lowest point, it lies 250 feet (76 m) below the seabed. High-speed TGV trains zoom through the Chunnel at speeds of 100 miles (161 km) per hour, and passengers can travel between London and Paris in less than three hours.

English Channel and nicknamed the Chunnel, it offers an important connection between France and England for both cars and trains.

France's state-owned railroad system also serves most cities and towns. In mountainous regions, where rail construction is difficult, buses connect train stations to remote villages. The high-speed TGV first ran between Paris and Lyon in 1983. The TGV carries passengers between many cities in modern France at speeds of more than 100 miles (161 km) per hour.

The two airports in the Paris region, Orly and Charles de Gaulle, are among the world's busiest. More than four hundred other airports are scattered around the country. Air France is the country's national airline, offering flights within France as well as internationally.

Water traffic also remains a feature of France's transportation system. The nation holds more than 5,000 miles (8,047 km) of rivers, canals, and other waterways that boats—depending on their size—can navigate. Along the French coasts, ports service sea traffic carrying passengers and freight.

◉ Media and Communications

France has a strong media network. More than eighty daily newspapers are published in France, helping keep residents up to date with news and other information. The papers with the most readers are *Le Figaro* and *Le Monde*—both national newspapers—and the Paris publication *Le Parisien*.

French listeners can tune in to dozens of radio stations to hear music, news, talk shows, and more. They also have their choice of a wide variety of television stations, including seven public stations and many more private options.

An estimated 30 million French people log on to the Internet for news, information, and entertainment. Many have access to the Internet at home. In addition, most of the nation's cities offer Internet cafés where people can get online.

Modern technology has also affected the way people get in touch with one another. Many French people use cellular phones in addition to or instead of older telephone lines. Approximately 35 million telephone landlines are in use around the country. By comparison, an estimated 55 million cell phones or more are in use in France.

The first French newspaper, *The Gazette*, was published in 1631.

The Future

Rising prices and high unemployment continue to plague the French economy. These problems have caused tension and unrest among French students and workers. The French people have sometimes used protests and strikes to express their dissatisfaction with the government. In addition, the nation faces social issues including culture clashes between different ethnic groups in France.

However, France's long history and strong tradition of democracy have given it many tools to deal with these problems. Its rich culture and its diverse population are also great assets. If France and its people can draw upon these resources to strengthen the nation from within, as well as to play a valuable part in the international community, the nation's future may well be as bright as its illustrious past.

Visit www.vgsbooks.com for links to websites with additional information and statistics about France's economy.

CA. 8000 B.C. Early people live in the area that later becomes France.

CA. 800 B.C. Celts invade France.

CA. 600 B.C. Greek settlers found the colony Massalia, which later becomes Marseille.

58 B.C. Roman general Julius Caesar invades France—then called Gaul—in an attempt to seize the area from the Celts.

52 B.C. Gaul becomes part of the Roman Empire.

A.D. 400S Various invaders, including the Visigoths, Franks, and Huns, attack Gaul.

714 Carolingian leader Charles Martel takes control of Francia.

800 Charles Martel becomes Charlemagne, ruler of the Holy Roman Empire.

987 The Carolingian dynasty ends, and Capetian rule begins.

1137 Louis VII marries Eleanor of Aquitaine.

1335 The Hundred Years' War begins.

1348 The Black Death breaks out in Marseille.

1429 Joan of Arc leads French forces in a victory over the English at Orléans.

EARLY 1500S The Renaissance brings a new age of artists and thinkers to France and across Europe. During this time, the Protestant Reformation also comes to France.

1598 Henry of Navarre grants religious freedom in France.

1648-1653 The Fronde rebellion rages across France.

1715 Five-year-old Louis XV inherits the French throne.

1789 The storming of the Bastille launches the French Revolution.

1793 Louis XVI and Marie-Antoinette are executed in Paris. The Louvre museum opens the same year.

1804 Napoléon Bonaparte declares himself emperor of France.

1815 Napoléon's British-led enemies defeat him at Waterloo, Belgium, and he is exiled to Saint Helena.

1862 Victor Hugo's *Les Misérables* is published.

1889 The Eiffel Tower is erected for the Paris World's Fair.

1914-1918 World War I rages in Europe.

1939	The first Cannes Film Festival is held.
1939-1945	World War II takes place.
1954-1962	The Algerian War rages, ending with Algeria's independence from France.
1968	Student demonstrations break out in Paris.
1983	The high-speed Train à Grande Vitesse (TGV) begins operation, connecting Paris and Lyon.
1993	France becomes one of the founding members of the European Union.
1994	The Eurotunnel, or Chunnel, opens as an underwater link between France and England.
1998	The French national soccer team wins the World Cup.
2000	Chinese-French writer Gao Xingjian wins the Nobel Prize in Literature.
2002	The euro officially replaces the French franc.
2003	A severe European heat wave kills thousands in France.
2005	Fatal fires break out in apartment buildings that house immigrant families. A few months later, two immigrant youths die and French police are accused of being involved. These incidents lead to widespread riots.
2008	French author J. M. G. Le Clézio wins the Nobel Prize in Literature.
2009	An Air France plane flying from Brazil to Paris crashes into the Atlantic Ocean, killing all 228 people aboard. The crash is the deadliest in Air France history.
2010	French athletes win eleven medals at the Winter Olympics in Vancouver, Canada.

COUNTRY NAME French Republic

AREA 211,209 square miles (547,029 sq. km)

MAIN LANDFORMS Aquitaine Lowlands, Brittany-Normandy Hills, Eastern Mountains (French Alps, Jura Mountains, Vosges Mountains), Massif Central, Northeastern Plateaus, Paris Basin, Pyrénées Mountains

HIGHEST POINT Mont Blanc, 15,771 feet (4,807 m) above sea level

LOWEST POINT Rhône River delta, 6.6 feet (2 m) below sea level

MAJOR RIVERS Escaut, Loire, Meuse, Moselle, Rhine, Rhône, Seine

ANIMALS Bass, bears, chamois, cranes, deer, foxes, genets, raccoon dogs, herons, perch, pheasants, pike, porcupines, trout, weasels, wild boars, wild horses, wild turkeys, wolves

CAPITAL CITY Paris

OTHER MAJOR CITIES Bordeaux, Lyon, Marseille, Nice, Strasbourg, Toulouse

OFFICIAL LANGUAGE French

MONETARY UNIT Euro. 100 cents = 1 euro.

FRENCH CURRENCY

The euro is the currency of France, along with fifteen other European Union nations. The process of conversion from the French franc to the euro began in 1999, when the euro was first introduced. The euro completely replaced the French franc in 2002. The franc had been used since the 1300s.

All countries that have adopted the euro share the same bills. The fronts of euro coins share the same images, while EU nations have created their own designs for the backs. All euro coins and bills are legal tender in every participating EU country.

Fast Facts

Currency

The French national flag consists of three vertical bands of color of equal width—blue, white, and red. The blue band is closest to the flagpole or staff. Because of its three-color nature, the French flag is sometimes called the tri-color, or the *drapeau tricolore*. The flag was adopted in 1794, in the midst of the French Revolution. The red and blue has traditionally represented Paris, while white stands for the French monarchy.

France's national anthem is called "La Marseillaise." A composer and army officer named Claude Joseph Rouget de Lisle wrote the words and music in 1792. The song was officially adopted as the nation's anthem in 1795. The first verse follows below in French and English.

Allons enfants de la Patrie,
Le jour de gloire est arrivé!
Contre nous de la tyrannie,
L'étandard sanglant est levé,
l'étandard sanglant est levé.
Entendez-vous dans la compagnes.
Mugir ces féroces soldats?
Ils viennent jusque dans nos bras
Égorger nos fils, nos compagnes!

Come, children of the Fatherland
The day of glory has arrived!
Against us, Tranny's
Bloody banner is raised,
Bloody banner is raised.
Do you hear in the countryside
Those ferocious soldiers roaring?
They come up to our arms
To slit the throats of our sons and wives!

 For a link to a site where you can listen to France's national anthem, "La Marseillaise," visit www.vgsbooks.com.

COCO CHANEL (1883–1971) Born in Saumur (in western France) as Gabrielle Bonheur, Chanel became famous as "Coco." She spent about six years of her childhood in an orphanage, where she learned to sew. Chanel went on to open her first clothing shop in Paris, and by the 1920s, she was a rising star in the world of fashion design. Chanel's trademark styles for women included sophisticated, tailored suits and chic black dresses. The fashion house she founded remains respected and influential. A movie about Chanel's life, starring French actress Audrey Tautou, came out in 2009.

ACHILLE-CLAUDE DEBUSSY (1862–1918) Debussy was born in Saint-Germain-en-Laye, near Paris. He took piano lessons as a boy and soon emerged as a major talent. He became a student at the Paris Conservatoire at the age of ten. He went on to teach in Russia and to study in Italy. Beginning in about the 1890s, he became a prolific composer. The style of many of his pieces was unconventional at the time. Music historians often link his work with the Impressionist style of painting, and he is regarded as one of France's most important composers.

J. M. G. LE CLÉZIO (b. 1940) Le Clézio—whose full name is Jean-Marie Gustave Le Clézio—was born in Nice. He began writing poetry as a boy and went to universities in both France and England to study literature and philosophy. For some time, he was a teacher in the United States. Later, he served in the French military in Thailand and Mexico. His works—which include novels, essays, short stories, and more—discuss topics including his childhood, travel, and exile. His body of work earned him the Nobel Prize in Literature in 2008.

AUGUSTE AND LOUIS LUMIÈRE (1862–1954 and 1864–1948) Born in Besançon, in eastern France, the Lumière brothers grew up working in their father's photography business. Together, the brothers went on to produce the *cinématographe*, a moving-picture camera, developer, and projector. Although another French inventor, Léon Bouly, had begun a similar project, the Lumières developed and improved the technology. The brothers demonstrated their invention in Paris in late 1895, showing ten films that were each less than one minute long. Many film historians regard the Lumières as the founders of modern cinema.

CLAUDE MONET (1840–1926) Born in Paris, Monet moved to Le Havre (in northwestern France) with his family when he was five years old. Monet's true love was art. As a student, he began selling his charcoal drawings. He later studied in Paris, where he met many other young artists. Together with painters including Alfred Sisley and Pierre-Auguste Renoir, he explored a new approach to painting that emphasized light, color, and movement over strict realism. The movement became known as Impressionism. Monet's personal life was often difficult, marked by poverty, the deaths of his first and second wives, and health problems. His artistic career was spectacular, however, and he created hundreds of works.

JEAN NOUVEL (b. 1945) Nouvel was born in Fumel, a village in south-western France. The son of two schoolteachers, he was a talented pupil. He attended the École des Beaux-Arts in Paris. While in school, he served as an assistant at an architecture firm before graduating and opening his own architecture studio. Some of Nouvel's most famous buildings include the Arab World Institute in Paris; the Agbar Tower in Barcelona, Spain; and the Guthrie Theater in Minneapolis, Minnesota. These and other works won him the prestigious Pritzker Prize in 2008.

ANTOINE DE SAINT-EXUPÉRY (1900–1944) Born in Lyon, Saint-Exupéry is best known for his short and beloved book *The Little Prince*, published in 1943. In addition to being an author, he was an accomplished aviator. *The Little Prince* was based in part on his experiences following an airplane crash in the Sahara. Saint-Exupéry worked as a pilot for the postal service and also flew for the French military. In 1944, during World War II, he disappeared over the Mediterranean Sea while on an information-gathering mission.

NICOLAS SARKOZY (b. 1955) Born in Paris, Sarkozy was elected as a city councillor of Neuilly-sur-Seine (a commune near Paris) at the age of twenty-two. In 1983 Sarkozy became Neuilly-sur-Seine's mayor, making him the youngest French mayor of a town of more than fifty thousand residents. His political career continued to gain strength when he joined the National Assembly in 1988. He went on to hold other prominent government positions, including minister of the interior and finance minister. In 2007 Sarkozy became France's twenty-third president and the first to have been born after World War II.

ZINEDINE ZIDANE (b. 1972) Widely viewed as one the world's most talented soccer players, Zidane was born in Marseille to Algerian immigrants. His talent was clear early in his life, and he played with junior soccer leagues during his teens. He went on to play for the French team AS Cannes, the Italian team Juventus, and the Spanish team Real Madrid. He was also a player for the French national team. Zidane retired from playing professionally in 2006, but he is still part of the soccer world as an adviser for Real Madrid.

LA CAMARGUE For nature lovers, La Camargue is a must-see spot in France. This region along France's southern coast is home to some of the nation's most diverse wildlife, as well as ecologically valuable wetlands. Part of the area is the Camargue Regional Nature Park, covering about 385 square miles (997 sq. km).

THE FRENCH ALPS For travelers who enjoy the outdoors, the French Alps are the perfect destination. Daytime activities include hiking, skiing, mountain climbing, visiting glaciers, and admiring stunning views. In the evenings, a variety of charming towns and villages offer lodging, as well as delicious French food.

MARSEILLE This lively seaside city is the oldest port in France and still a vibrant center with a diverse population. Its attractions include bustling markets, museums showcasing everything from ancient Roman history to modern art, and some of the nation's best seafood.

NICE This glistening city on the French Riviera offers sandy beaches, luxurious resorts, and lots of sunshine. Visitors can also enjoy strolling through attractive squares, touring a variety of museums, or simply sitting at cafés and watching the world go by.

NORMANDY History buffs won't want to miss Normandy's landing beaches, the site of the pivotal World War II D-day invasion by the Allies. Along the beaches lie memorials to the tens of thousands of soldiers who died here. A huge cemetery lies at Colleville-sur-Mer, and visitors can see several museums. Also in Normandy is Mont Saint-Michel, an abbey (a building occupied by a community of monks) whose origins date back about one thousand years. In addition to its historical interest, the abbey is a natural beauty. At low tide, mudflats stretch between the abbey and the mainland. But at high tide, Mont Saint-Michel becomes a tiny island, connected to shore only by a single raised road.

PALACE OF VERSAILLES Lying about 14 miles (23 km) southwest of Paris, the Palace of Versailles was once home to French royalty. The palace is now a museum, and its lavishly decorated rooms, wealth of artwork, and lush gardens are a popular attraction for visitors from around the world.

PARIS As the French capital and also its cultural center, Paris offers sights to suit every traveler. Architecture buffs will rush to see the Eiffel Tower, the amazing Gothic cathedral Notre Dame, and Jean Nouvel's Arab World Institute. Shoppers can find their hearts' desires in the city's many fashionable boutiques or in quirky flea markets. Art lovers won't want to miss the Louvre or the Musée d'Orsay, and a trip to the top of the Arc de Triomphe or the Eiffel Tower offers magnificent views of Paris—often called the City of Lights.

colony: a territory ruled and occupied by a foreign power

dynasty: a family of rulers

European Union (EU): an organization of European countries that promotes cooperation among its members in matters of politics and economics

gross domestic product (GDP): a measure of the total value of goods and services produced within a country's boundaries in a certain amount of time (usually one year), regardless of the citizenship of the producers

immigrant: someone who arrives to live in a new country

industrialization: the shift from an economy based on farming to one based on manufacturing

inflation: rapidly rising prices, usually paired with a decrease in the value of a nation's currency

Islam: a religion founded on the Arabian Peninsula in the seventh century A.D. by the prophet Muhammad

literacy: the ability to read and write a basic sentence. A country's literacy rate is one indicator of its level of human development.

monarchy: a government headed by a leader such as a king, queen, or prince, with titles usually passed down in the family through the generations. Some monarchs hold complete power, while others share their power with other government officials.

mosque: an Islamic place of worship

Orthodox Christianity: also called Eastern Orthodoxy, this religion is a branch of Christianity that broke off from the Roman Catholic Church in 1054

privatization: the transfer of ownership of businesses, goods, and other assets from government (public) to individual (private) control

Protestantism: the general name for hundreds of non-Catholic Christian sects and denominations

Roman Catholicism: a branch of Christianity headed by the pope and based in Vatican City in Rome, Italy

Selected Bibliography

British Broadcasting Corporation. BBC News—Europe. 2009.
http://news.bbc.co.uk/2/hi/europe/default.stm (August 1, 2009).
This news site provides a range of up-to-date information and archived articles about France and the surrounding region.

Cable News Network. CNN.com International. 2009. http://edition .cnn.com/WORLD/ (August 3, 2009).
CNN offers plenty of information on current events and breaking news in France, as well as a searchable archive of older articles.

Clarke, Stephen. *Talk to the Snail: Ten Commandments for Understanding the French*. New York: Bloomsbury, 2006.
This book takes a humorous look at French culture and life, from the perspective of a British author who has lived in France for more than a decade.

***Europa World Yearbook*, 2008. Vol. 2. London: Europa Publications, 2008.**
Covering France's recent history, economy, and government, this annual publication also provides a wealth of statistics on population, employment, trade, and more.

***The International Year Book and Statesmen's Who's Who*. London: Burke's Peerage, 2007.**
An annually released reference material, this book provides information on France's economy, politics, people, and more.

New York Times Company. The *New York Times* on the Web. 2008.
http://www.nytimes.com (August 12, 2009).
This online version of the newspaper offers current news stories along with an archive of articles on France.

"PRB 2009 World Population Data Sheet." Population Reference Bureau (PRB). 2009. http://www.prb.org (August 13, 2009).
This annual statistics sheet provides a wealth of data on France's population, birth rates and death rates, fertility rate, infant mortality rate, and other useful demographic information.

Turner, Barry, ed. *The Statesman's Yearbook: The Politics, Cultures, and Economies of the World, 2009*. New York: Macmillan Press, 2008.
This resource provides concise information on France's history, climate, government, economy, and culture, including relevant statistics.

UNICEF. "At a Glance: France." UNICEF: Information by Country. 2009. http://www.unicef.org/infobycountry/france.html (August 12, 2009).
This site from the United Nations agency UNICEF offers details about education, nutrition, and other demographics in France.

U.S. Department of State. "2008 Human Rights Report: France." U.S. Department of State: Country Reports on Human Rights Practices. 2009. http://www.state.gov/g/drl/rls/hrrpt/2008/eur/119079.htm (August 9, 2009).
This website is published by the U.S. State Department's Bureau of Democracy, Human Rights, and Labor. It provides a yearly update on the human rights situation within France, including concerns about women's rights, treatment of ethnic minorities, and other issues.

World Health Organization. "France." World Health Organization: Countries. 2009. http://www.who.int/countries/fra/en/ (August 3, 2009).
This website provides a wealth of statistics and information on health issues in France.

Abrams, Dennis. *Nicolas Sarkozy.* **New York: Chelsea House, 2009.**
Learn more about France's twenty-third president.

Arnold, James R. *The Aftermath of the French Revolution.* **Minneapolis: Twenty-First Century Books, 2009.**
Learn more about the dramatic changes that took place in France following the French Revolution.

Day, Nancy. *Your Travel Guide to Renaissance Europe.* **Minneapolis: Twenty-First Century Books, 2001.**
Take a trip back in time to explore France and other European nations during the Renaissance.

Donovan, Sandy. *The Channel Tunnel.* **Minneapolis: Lerner Publications Company, 2003.**
This entry in the Great Building Feats series describes the history, politics, and engineering surrounding the creation of the undersea tunnel linking France and England.

Greene, Meg. *The Eiffel Tower.* **San Diego: Lucent Books, 2001.**
Discover the history and science behind one of the world's most amazing structures.

Kallen, Stuart A. *Claude Monet.* **Farmington Hills, MI: Lucent Books, 2009.**
Explore the life and work of Monet, who was a prominent member of the Impressionist movement and remains one of France's most famous and popular artists.

Kerns, Ann. *Seven Wonders of Architecture.* **Minneapolis: Twenty-First Century Books, 2010.**
This book details seven of the world's architectural wonders, including a chapter on the Eiffel Tower.

Kramer, Ann. *Eleanor of Aquitaine: The Queen Who Rode Off to Battle.* **Washington, DC: National Geographic, 2006.**
Eleanor of Aquitaine was one of the wealthiest and most powerful women of the Middle Ages. Learn more about her life and times in this book.

Landau, Elaine. *Napoleon Bonaparte.* **Minneapolis: Twenty-First Century Books, 2006.**
Explore the life and times of one of France's most famous military commanders and onetime emperor.

Lebovitz, David. "David Lebovitz: Living the Sweet Life in Paris."
http://www.davidlebovitz.com/
A former chef at a popular Berkeley, California, restaurant and a regular contributor to various food magazines, Lebovitz moved to France in 2002. In his mouthwatering blog, he shares his experiences of living, eating, and cooking as an American in Paris.

Lonely Planet: France
http://www.lonelyplanet.com/france
Visit this website for information about traveling to France. You can also learn some background information about the country at this site.

Lüsted, Marcia Amidon. *The Chunnel*. Detroit: Thomson/Gale, 2005.
Building the Chunnel was an amazing feat of engineering. Discover more about it in this book.

Metcalf, Tom. *Nuclear Power*. Detroit: Greenhaven Press, 2007.
France is a leading producer of nuclear power. This book examines this energy source.

Palace of Versailles
http://en.chateauversailles.fr/homepage
Even if you can't make it to France, you can still take a virtual tour of the magnificent Palace of Versailles. This official website provides history, photographs, and videos about the former royal residence.

Rawlins, Carol. *The Seine River*. New York: Franklin Watts, 2001.
Take a journey down France's Seine River, which flows through Paris and beyond.

vgsbooks.com
http://www.vgsbooks.com
Visit vgsbooks.com, the home page of the Visual Geography Series®. You can get linked to all sorts of useful online information, including geographical, historical, demographic, cultural, and economic websites. The vgsbooks.com site is a great resource for late-breaking news and statistics.

Waldee, Lynne Marie. *Cooking the French Way*. Minneapolis: Lerner Publishing Company, 2002.
This cookbook presents a selection of recipes from France, including potato-and-leek soup, sautéed chicken, and crepes with fresh strawberries.

Wilkinson, Philip. *Joan of Arc: The Teenager Who Saved Her Nation*. Washington, DC: National Geographic Society, 2007.
Find out more about the life of Joan of Arc, a national heroine and patron saint of France.

Captions for photos appearing on cover and chapter openers:

Cover: The Arc de Triomphe is located at the western end of the Champs-Élysées in Paris. The arch honors those who fought for France, particularly during the Napoleonic Wars (1803–1815).

pp. 4–5 Boats dot the blue waters of the Mediterranean Sea off the coast of southeastern France.

pp. 8–9 A view of a snow-covered Mont Blanc can be seen across the flower-covered slopes of another peak in the French Alps.

pp. 18–19 More than three thousand stones erected by prehistoric peoples stand near the town of Carnac in Brittany, France. Scientists date them to about 4,500 to 3,300 B.C.

pp. 38–39 A customer buys a baguette (loaf of French bread) from a baker at an open-air market in Paris.

pp. 46–47 Notre-Dame de Reims (Our Lady of Rheims) is a Roman Catholic cathedral in Rheims. It was built at the end of the 1200s to replace an even older church that burned down. Shown in this photo is the back of the cathedral and the surrounding gardens.

pp. 58–59 Grape vineyards cover the rolling lands of Provence, France. The region of Provence is well known for its cuisine and its wines.

Photo Acknowledgments

The images in this book are used with the permission of: © Robert Harding Picture Library/SuperStock, pp. 4–5, 8–9, 58–59; © XNR Productions, pp. 6, 10; © Harald Sund/Stone/Getty Images, p. 11; © Travel Library Limited/SuperStock, p. 12; © age fotostock/SuperStock, pp. 14, 52; © Helene Rogers/Art Directors & TRIP, pp. 16, 60; © Chris Wormald/Art Directors & TRIP, pp. 18–19; © Bob Turner/Art Directors & TRIP, pp. 20, 46–47; © Mansell/Time & Life Pictures/Getty Images, p. 21; © Anthony Frederick Augustus Sandys/The Bridgeman Art Library/Getty Images, p. 22; © Sir John Gilbert/The Bridgeman Art Library/Getty Images, p. 24; © Imagno/Hulton Archive/Getty Images, pp. 26, 50 (right); © Popperfoto/Getty Images, p. 27; © Peter Willi/SuperStock, p. 28; © Apic/Hulton Archive/Getty Images, p. 31; © De Agostini/SuperStock, p. 33; AP Photo, p. 34; AP Photo/Bettina Rheims, p. 35; © Saul Loeb/AFP/Getty Images, p. 36; © Pictures Colour Library/Alamy, pp. 38–39; © Directphoto.org/Alamy, p. 40; © Alex Bartel/Art Directors & TRIP, p. 41; © Stephane De Sakutin/AFP/Getty Images, pp. 42, 48; © Image Source/Getty Images, p. 43; © David W. Hamilton/The Image Bank/Getty Images, p. 44; © Stanislas Merlin/Getty Images, p. 45; AP Photo/Michel Spingler, p. 49; © Stock Montage/Hulton Archive/Getty Images, p. 50 (left); © Lipnitzki/Roger Viollet/Getty Images, pp. 51, 53; © Macduff Everton/The Image Works, p. 52 (inset); © Bertrand Guay/AFP/Getty Images, p. 54; AP Photo/Christophe Ena, p. 57; © Photononstop/SuperStock, p. 62; © Denis Charlet/AFP/Getty Images, p. 64; © Flirt/SuperStock, p. 68; © Laura Westlund/Independent Picture Service, p. 69.

Front cover: © Mark Segal/Digital Vision/Getty Images.